O'C<
The Iris

SUPPLEMENT

O'Connor's
The Irish Notary

SUPPLEMENT

Eamonn G. Hall
and
E. Rory O'Connor

WITH A FOREWORD BY

The Hon. Mr. Justice John L. Murray
Chief Justice of Ireland

THE FACULTY OF NOTARIES PUBLIC IN IRELAND
2007

First Published 2007 by the Faculty of Notaries Public in Ireland,
34 Upper Baggot Street, Dublin 4.

© Eamonn G. Hall and E. Rory O'Connor, 2007

All rights reserved. No part of this publication may be reproduced or transmitted in any form or by any means, electronic, mechanical, photocopying, recording or otherwise or stored in any retrieval system without the written permission of the copyright holders for the time being to be applied for through the publisher.

Typeset by Kathy Kelly

Printed by Future Print Ltd.

ISBN 978-0-9505012-0-8

DISCLAIMER

The views expressed in this publication are those of the authors and contributors respectively unless otherwise expressly stated. Such views, and the forms and precedents included in the work, have been prepared as a guide for notaries public and legal practitioners, and for law graduates intending to take the Faculty examination leading to appointment as a notary public. Such views, forms and precedents are not intended as legal advice and shall not be used by any person as a substitute for such advice.

CONTENTS

	Page
Foreword	ix
Acknowledgements	xi
1. INTRODUCTION	1
2. THE OFFICE OF NOTARY	3
3. QUALIFICATIONS FOR THE OFFICE OF NOTARY	6
4. APPLICATION FOR APPOINTMENT	9
5. CONDUCT OF A NOTARY	10
6. NOTARIAL ACCOUTREMENTS	17
7. OATHS: SUBSTANCE, FORM AND PROCEDURE	22
8. STRUCTURE OF CERTAIN LEGAL DOCUMENTS: POWER OF ATTORNEY: ENDURING POWER OF ATTORNEY	26
9. SHIPS PROTESTS	34
10. BILLS OF EXCHANGE	40
11. LEGALISATION AND THE APOSTILLE	42
12. FOREIGN ADOPTION: THE ROLE OF THE NOTARY PUBLIC	57
13. MONEY-LAUNDERING	65

14. ELECTRONIC COMMERCE	71
APPENDICES	77
TABLE OF STATUTES	104
INDEX	107

Note: The material in Chapters 1 to 11 is by way of addendum to the corresponding chapters in the principal work. The material in Chapter 8 (Powers of Attorney) and in Chapters 12 to 14 is new.

The Authors

Eamonn G. Hall is chief solicitor of Eircom, an examiner in constitutional law and consultant in judicial review to the law school of the Law Society. A graduate of UCD, UCG and TCD with degrees of BA, LLB and PhD, he qualified as a solicitor in 1974 and subsequently as a Notary Public. A former president of the Medico-Legal Society of Ireland, past chairman of the Irish Society for European Law and the Incorporated Council of Law Reporting for Ireland, he served for three years as a member of the first Information Society Commission. He is a Fellow of the Society for Advanced Legal Studies (London) and a Visiting Fellow and member of the Adjunct School of Law at UCD. Author of *The Electronic Age: Telecommunication in Ireland* (1993), Dr. Hall was consultant editor of the *Irish Digest 1994-1999*, has served as the chairman of the editorial board of the Law Society's *Gazette* and has contributed chapters and articles to various publications, nationally and internationally.

E. Rory O'Connor, author of the principal work, *The Irish Notary* (Professional Books, 1987) is Dean of the Faculty of Notaries Public in Ireland and has been practising as a Notary Public for over 25 years. Having qualified as a solicitor (1953) and awarded the Overend Scholarship of the Law Society of Ireland, Rory O'Connor practised as a solicitor in Clare and Waterford for a number of years before entering the banking service in Dublin as a legal adviser. He was Law Agent and General Counsel to the Allied Irish Banks Group for over 30 years. Rory O'Connor is the author of many works on banking law and practice including *The Law and Practice in Ireland Relating to Cheques and Analogous Instruments* (The Institute of Bankers, 1993). For his contribution to the advancement of education in banking he was elected a Fellow of the Institute of Bankers in Ireland.

FOREWORD

It gives me great pleasure to welcome this Supplement to *The Irish Notary*. Two decades after it was first published, this book continues to provide an invaluable insight into the work and role of the notary, a position that is of prime importance in a modern, expanding economy. The Supplement is particularly useful given the numerous changes in notarial practice that have taken place in recent years, most notably with Ireland's ratification in 1999 of the Hague Convention of 5 October 1961.

The increasing interaction between legal systems, economies and individuals, not only in the European Union but in the wider international context, underscored by the continuous expansion in Irish investment abroad, means that the functions fulfilled by the notary are of ever-increasing significance. This fact is amply attested to in this Supplement, dealing as it does with such matters as foreign adoption, money-laundering and electronic commerce, not dealt with in the original work.

The authors rightly emphasise that in order to provide a service that can be trusted and afforded recognition worldwide, Irish notaries must demonstrate probity and integrity, and satisfy the highest professional standards. This Supplement to the principal work will no doubt assist in maintaining high standards, and provide an indispensable reference work for all notaries in Ireland.

The Hon. Mr. Justice John L. Murray
Chief Justice of Ireland
Four Courts
Dublin 7

ACKNOWLEDGEMENTS

The authors wish to thank those colleagues who encouraged them to write this Supplement. Their helpful advice, material and suggestions were much appreciated. In particular, the authors wish to thank: The Hon. Mr. Justice John L. Murray, the Chief Justice of Ireland, for writing the Foreword to the Supplement in which he recognises the significant role of the Notary Public in international exchanges and in the economic, commercial and social life of the State; David A. Walsh, Solicitor and Notary Public, for contributing the text of Chapter 12, Foreign Adoption; Gerard F. Griffin, Solicitor and Notary Public, for contributing the text of Chapter 13, Money-laundering; Kathy Kelly who type-set the manuscript, for her guidance on presentation of material; Brendan Walsh, Registrar of the Faculty of Notaries Public in Ireland for his encouragement and unremitting pressure to produce the work; the AIB Group for their generous financial support of the publication and the Registrar and staff of the Supreme Court Office for their assistance in producing elusive material.

Eamonn G. Hall
E. Rory O'Connor
February 2007

Chapter 1

INTRODUCTION

In the years that have passed since the publication, in 1987, of *The Irish Notary*, notarial practice in Ireland has undergone many changes. Some of these changes have been influenced by frequent dialogue and other exchanges between the Faculty of Notaries Public in Ireland and other notarial bodies in Europe and North America but principally the United Kingdom Notarial Forum, the Notaries Society and the Scriveners' Company of London. Ireland's ratification, in 1999, of the Convention Abolishing the Requirement of Legalisation for Foreign Public Documents concluded at The Hague on 5 October 1961 ('The Hague Convention of 5 October 1961') introduced long awaited change in practice relating to legalisation. Under the Convention, the Apostille certificate may be used between countries that have signed, ratified or acceded to the Convention in place of the cumbersome system of legalisation. Legalisation, however, remains necessary when the country in which a public document is to be received or from which it emanates, is not a signatory to, or does not otherwise recognise, the Convention or the Convention Abolishing the legalisation of documents in Member States of the European Communities concluded 25 May 1987.

Other changes in practice have come about as a result of recommendations made by the Faculty in order to safeguard the interests of the Irish notary and to preserve the integrity of the notarial act on documents processed in Ireland for use abroad.

There have been changes also in the area of banking practice where the use of irrevocable letters of credit and electronic payment systems in foreign trade settlements have substantially replaced foreign bills of exchange and promissory notes. We have also seen the demise of the historical days of grace in relation to the calculation of time for payment of foreign bills.

As powers of attorney represent an important part of the work of a notary public, Chapter 8 of the principal work has been updated and reflects changes in the law introduced by the Powers of Attorney Act, 1996 and incorporates a comprehensive review of the Enduring Power of Attorney which was envisaged but not incorporated into Irish law when the principal work was published.

In addition to updating the principal work, new chapters on foreign adoption, money-laundering and electronic commerce have been added as well as a collection of new precedents.

In 1993, regulations governing the admission of persons to act as notaries public were made pursuant to the Rules of the Superior Courts (No. 2) of 1993. In 2005 and 2006 Directions were made by the Chief Justice which affect the practice in relation to applications for appointment as notaries public and the conduct of notaries following their appointment.

In identifying the changes that have occurred since the publication of the principal work, the supplement's authors have followed the same chapter titles as in the principal work.

Chapter 2

THE OFFICE OF NOTARY

Notarial Acts; Public Acts and Private Acts

In Chapter 2 of the principal work reference is made to 'notarial acts' and the expression is briefly explained in a footnote drawing on Brooke's Notary[1]. In this supplement it is proposed to offer further explanation regarding the meaning and usage of the expression 'notarial act'.

In countries that follow the common law legal system, the word 'act' in the expression 'notarial act' bears a meaning broadly corresponding with the French word *actes*, meaning 'instrument', used in countries which follow the civil law code. In civil law countries, where notaries (sometimes described as the Latin notaries) are an integral and indispensable part of the legal system, the civil law code gives the notary a special place in the legal hierarchy. It also accords a unique status on the notarial act clothing it with *publica fides* (absolute public faith) and rendering it self-probative as respects the transaction, facts and matters therein recorded. In contrast, while in common law countries the office of notary is highly respected, neither the notary public nor the notarial act enjoys a comparable status to the civil law notary. This has to do largely with the different ways in which the office of notary public developed in mainland Europe and in post-Reformation England. In England (and Ireland) a different approach was adopted as regards the appointment and empowering of notaries public, leaving it largely to the common law, custom and usage to determine the extent of the notary's powers and functions. The profession did not develop, therefore, on the same lines as, for example, the French notaire, the German notar or the Spanish notario and other notaries within the civil law system. While notaries public, as the third branch of an unintegrated legal profession in Ireland, may not

---

[1] *Brooke's Treatise on the Office of a Notary of England* (9th Edition) by J. Charlesworth, reprinted 1985, (Sweet & Maxwell); see also *Brooke's Notary* (11th Edition) by Nigel Ready (1992) Sweet & Maxwell and later editions.

enjoy the same 'exalted' status as that of notaries in civil law countries, they perform a most important and essential function for the benefit of the legal profession, the commercial community and the country in general; and their acts, and the matters to which they give testimony, are almost universally accepted, without further proof.

A notarial act may be defined as an instrument constituted by the affixing of a notary's signature and seal of office to a document in verification of its authenticity or its execution, or of some material fact or matter therein recorded. The notarial act may take the form of an instrument made by the notary public alone e.g. deed poll, certificate or declaration, or it may be by way of an attestation by the notary of the execution of a document by another person or persons e.g. power of attorney. Most frequently, the notarial act will be in the form of a certificate executed by the notary public attached to or endorsed on a document produced to the notary for the purpose of being notarised. It can be said that the effect of a notarial act on a document is to enhance the probity and acceptance of the notarised document. It is, therefore, of the utmost importance that notaries exercise the greatest care and diligence in providing such acts. A slipshod approach in such matters could not only reflect adversely on the notary and the Faculty, but on the State as well. Copies of notarial acts must be kept by the notary.

Notarial acts may be public acts or private acts. In countries that follow the civil law system, the notarial acts are public acts. In common law countries, notarial acts are invariably private acts in the absence of a legislative framework giving special recognition to such acts. Though there is no substantial difference in form between the two types of notarial act, the public act is regarded in civil law countries as superior and often indispensable for executory purposes. Notarial acts in private form have no lesser value in probative terms and provide a very important function in the commercial life of the State.

Components of a Notarial Act

The components of a notarial act are: (1) the notary's full name, which must correspond with the name on the notary's official seal; (2) the name and address of the appearer (if any) and the means by which the appearer's identity was established; (3) a description of the document or matter being notarised; (4) the appearer's signature, where applicable; (5) the place at which the act is done, which confirms locus and jurisdiction; (6) the date on which the notarial act is done, specifying the month in writing and not in figures; (7) the notary's signature, which must be his or her usual or customary signature, and (8) the notary's official seal. The components of the notarial act will not necessarily follow the foregoing sequence. The notarial act usually begins with a reference to the date and place and the name of the notary but all components must be present in the completed act.

Public acts (and private acts) of a notary must not be confused with 'public documents' (*actes publics*) as defined in the Convention Abolishing the Requirement of Legalisation for Foreign Public Documents concluded at The Hague on 5 October 1961 ('the Convention'), though the two may overlap on occasions e.g. a notarial act. Under Article 1 of the Convention, the following are deemed public documents for the purposes of the Convention:

(a) documents emanating from an authority or an official connected with the courts or tribunals of the State, including those emanating from a public prosecutor, a clerk of a court or process-server (hussier de justice);
(b) administrative documents;
(c) notarial acts;
(d) official certificates which are placed on documents signed by persons in their private capacity, such as official certificates recording the registration of a document or the fact that it was in existence on a certain date and official and notarial authentications of signature.

It will be noted with reference to the category of documents described at (d) above that the recognition accorded by the Convention is to the official certificates placed on the documents and not to the documents themselves. Unless notarised, documents of an administrative nature but dealing directly with commercial or customs operations e.g. certificates of origin of goods, import and export licences are excluded from the scope of the Convention.

The reader is referred to Chapter 11 of the supplement, which deals with legalisation and the apostille, and to Appendix 2 of the principal work which contains the full text, in English, of the Hague Convention.

Chapter 3

QUALIFICATIONS FOR OFFICE OF NOTARY

The Faculty of Notaries Public in Ireland considers that a person aspiring to be appointed a notary public should be a qualified solicitor with significant post-qualification experience in commercial or mercantile law, international law and conveyancing. This general criterion substantially reflects the stance of Finlay C.J. in *Re Timothy McCarthy* [1990] ILRM 84, 86 in which he expressed the view that even where the applicant is a fully qualified solicitor, he or she should preferably have a significant number of years of experience as such. Though persons other than solicitors have, from time to time, been appointed notaries in Ireland, at the pleasure of the Chief Justice e.g. barristers in industry, this is now a rare occurrence and, invariably, in such cases the appointee will possess a recognised qualification in law and will have had considerable relevant experience in a commercial field. The requirement for an applicant to obtain a certificate of competency from the Faculty ensures that the standard of entry into the notarial profession will be maintained at a high level into the future.

Certificate of Competency

The Rules of the Superior Courts (No. 2) of 1993 (S.I. No. 265 of 1993), which came into operation on 9 September 1993, added Order 127 to the Rules of the Superior Courts. The 1993 Order gives the Chief Justice, 'in the exercise of his discretion and from time to time', power to make such rules and regulations or give such practice directions as he may think fit as to the form and mode of application to be appointed a notary public. The Order further provides that such rules, regulations or directions may require that the applicant satisfy the Chief Justice, in advance of being appointed, that he or she has the requisite and appropriate knowledge of notarial practice and procedure. In pursuance of the Order, the Chief Justice on 28 March 1994 made directions and regulations the effect of which may be paraphrased as follows:

1. Before making application to the Chief Justice to be appointed a notary public, the applicant is required to satisfy the Faculty of Notaries Public in Ireland ('the Faculty') that he or she has a sufficient knowledge of notarial matters and procedures and of the particular legal provisions applicable to notarial matters to be a competent and efficient person to carry out the duties of a notary public, if appointed.
2. An applicant who fails to obtain a certificate of competency from the Faculty, may request a statement in writing from the Faculty giving the reasons for declining to grant such certificate.
3. An applicant for appointment who has failed to obtain a certificate of competency from the Faculty may, nevertheless, continue with his or her application but, in such circumstances, must exhibit on affidavit the decision of the Faculty and the reasons given by the Faculty for declining to grant such certificate. On such application the applicant may adduce other evidence upon which the applicant intends to rely in regard to his or her competency.

The Examination Body of the Faculty of Notaries Public in Ireland conducts examinations for the purposes of Order 127 of the Rules of the Superior Courts as occasion arises and, based on the results of such examinations, makes recommendations to the Faculty as regards the issuing of the certificates of competency. The full texts of Order 127 and the Direction are set out in Appendix 1 and 1A to the supplement. A form of Certificate of Competency is contained in Appendix 1B. The syllabus for the Faculty examination includes:-

(1) History of the Notary Public in Ireland
(2) Ethics
(3) Private International Law
(4) Company Law
(5) Mercantile Law: Bills of Exchange: Noting and Protesting of bills
(6) Ships Protests
(7) The Hague Convention of 5 October 1961 and other EU Conventions relevant to Notaries Public
(8) Powers of Attorney: Enduring Powers of Attorney

(9) Foreign Adoption (Inter-country Adoption), and
(10) Money-laundering legislation

A copy of the syllabus and a study plan may be obtained by writing to the Registrar, The Faculty of Notaries Public, 34 Upper Baggot Street, Dublin 4.

Chapter 4

APPLICATION FOR APPOINTMENT

Prior to 2005, a person applying to be appointed a notary public was required to establish, to the satisfaction of the Chief Justice, that there was an immediate need for the appointment of a notary public in the area i.e. county, city or district, for which the applicant was seeking to be appointed. This need might have been justified by the fact that there was no notary practising in or within a reasonable distance from the area for which appointment was sought, the death or incapacity of a notary or because demand for the services of an additional notary had arisen due to substantial growth in commercial activity in the area. On 25 January 2006, the Chief Justice, following consultation with the Faculty of Notaries Public in Ireland, made a Direction dispensing with the requirement to show need. As a consequence, it is no longer necessary for the applicant to make reference in his or her Petition, or in the supporting certificates of solicitors and business persons, to the need for such appointment. The applicant, however, should state in the Petition that the appointment, if made, would operate for the greater convenience and accommodation of the public in the area to which the application relates. This is, historically, the *raison d'être* of the office of notary public. Furthermore, since 2 October 2006, pursuant to a Direction of the Chief Justice, an applicant is required to provide an appropriate undertaking to observe the Code of Conduct of The Faculty of Notaries Public in Ireland (adopted 21 November, 1986) and such rules, regulations and bye-laws governing the professional practice and procedure of notaries public in Ireland, and the standards to be observed by them, as shall from time to time be made and published by the Faculty. In all other respects, the procedure is as set out in the principal work but notice of application is not now required to be served on notaries public practising in counties adjoining the county to which the application relates.

The Directions of the Chief Justice and specimen forms of Petition, Affidavit verifying the Petition, Certificates of Fitness and Notice of Motion are contained in Appendix 2 to 2F to this supplement.

Chapter 5

CONDUCT OF A NOTARY

Proof of Identity

In the principal work, the importance of obtaining proper identification of persons appearing before a notary public to avail of the notary's services was emphasised and appropriate guidance offered. Such are the changes that have occurred in Irish society in the intervening years that it is now considered appropriate to revisit the subject.

In transactions having a foreign element, production of a current valid passport is almost universally the accepted means of identification. Meeting such a requirement is unlikely to create any inconvenience as, invariably, a person seeking a notary's services will be doing so in connection with a transaction likely to involve foreign travel, for which a passport will be required. Where, however, the appearer does not hold a passport e.g. a refugee, asylum seeker or migrant worker, other means of identification will have to be used. Such means may include production of a national identity card issued by the authorities of an EU Member State, the Swiss Confederation, or a contracting party to the Agreement on the European Economic Area signed at Oporto on 2 May 1992 ('the EEA'), or a travel document issued under section 4 of the Refugee Act, 1996 or, other form of travel document issued by the State for limited purposes. Each of these documents will contain a photograph of the holder with which his or her facial appearance may be compared. A driving licence is not generally regarded as adequate proof of identity in the context of a foreign transaction. This is because of the large numbers of bogus driving licences currently in circulation throughout Europe. A driving licence may, cautiously, be accepted for purely domestic purposes if tendered with proof of residence in the form of a utility bill or bank statement (preferably not more than three months old) addressed to the appearer at the address of the appearer stated in the document to be notarised.

Understanding the Document

A notary public, who is requested to attest a signature to a document, must be satisfied that the appearer has legal capacity and understands the nature and legal significance of the document before allowing it to be executed. Though a notary public, *qua* notary, may not be the appearer's legal adviser, he or she, nevertheless, has a duty to ensure that the appearer understands the significance of the transaction being entered into. The notary is a professional service provider and, as such, assumes the common law duties arising from that particular relationship. If it transpires that the appearer does not understand the nature of the document, or the significance of the transaction, it is the duty of the notary to caution the appearer not to sign the document until the appearer has received proper advice. The adage that 'a notary's duty is to the document and not to the signatory' is unlikely to meet with judicial favour in modern times.

Documents in Foreign Languages: Purchase of Foreign Property

Thousands of Irish citizens invest substantial monies annually in the acquisition of overseas properties. These may be intended for use as permanent residences or holiday homes. Such investments frequently result from newspaper advertisements and exhibitions sponsored by foreign developers or estate agents acting on their behalf in Ireland. Any advice, information or representation received by an investor from such sources may not be independent and has the potential to give rise to conflicts of interest. Furthermore, the legal work necessary to vest title in the investor may be carried out by a foreign lawyer engaged on the investor's behalf by the estate agent or the developer. The investor may not in fact physically meet the foreign lawyer in the course of the entire transaction. This is because, in most of these transactions, the foreign lawyer is empowered to act on the investor's behalf under a power of attorney executed by the investor in Ireland. In general, these investors do not employ Irish solicitors to represent them, either directly or through the solicitors' foreign agents. They appear to be satisfied to act on information and advice given to them by the property developers or their agents; an attitude completely, and inexplicably, at variance with the attitude such persons would adopt when buying property in Ireland.

An Irish notary's introduction to a transaction involving the acquisition of foreign property frequently begins against a background such as described above when the investor, now described as a purchaser, attends before the notary in order to have documents notarised. These documents will, invariably, include a power of attorney. The power of attorney will frequently be written in a foreign language and a translation may or may not be included. The notary is requested to witness the purchaser's signature to the power of attorney and provide a formal attestation as a notarial act. In the exercise of his or her function the notary must act with the greatest care and circumspection for the following reasons:

1. Though the notary may not be the purchaser's legal adviser, nevertheless, as a service provider, he or she has a duty of care to the appearer. A fundamental part of that duty is to establish that the appearer has legal capacity and understands the nature and significance of the document before it is executed.

2. The notary may not possess a competent knowledge of the language in which the power of attorney is written and, consequently, in the absence of a translation in English, will not be in a position to read or explain the document to the appearer; and even where a translation in English is supplied, the notary will not be able to say, without confirmation from a language expert, that such translation is accurate and complete.

3. The notary is unlikely to know anything about the purchaser's financial circumstances or his or her ability to understand the various implications of the transaction e.g. legal, taxation and financial.

The Association of Chartered Accountants has recently[2] issued a strongly worded warning to Irish persons contemplating buying property in foreign countries, particularly countries outside the EU, without first having the taxation implications of the transaction professionally investigated. Examples given of matters that require to be investigated are:

- Whether a double taxation agreement between Ireland and the foreign country is in place;

---

[2] *Irish Independent* 21 July 2006

- If it is, to what taxes does it extend i.e., does it cover capital gains tax, income tax, inheritance tax, wealth tax and deemed income;
- Is interest paid on a foreign mortgage tax deductible, and
- Is a service charge payable and to whom; and is the service charge deductible.

The Association advises that intending purchasers seek independent taxation advice on these matters before proceeding with the purchase. The Faculty of Notaries endorses that advice. Notaries involved in completing documents in connection with foreign property acquisitions should raise the taxation issue with the appearer and recommend that he or she seek independent taxation advice. (See further in this chapter under 'Acknowledgment Letter'.)

Translations
Where a foreign lawyer, representing an Irish citizen in a foreign property transaction, furnishes an English translation of the power of attorney with the original foreign language document, the notary public in Ireland before whom the purchaser appears may accept and act on such translation. This is justified by the rules of professional etiquette in international transactions. If, however, the notary has serious misgivings in regard to the translation, he or she may request the purchaser to obtain a letter of confirmation from a qualified language translator in Ireland or the United Kingdom or, alternatively, obtain the purchaser's written authority for the notary to organise verification of the translation. English language translations of foreign language documents, furnished by foreign lawyers, are found frequently to contain spelling and grammatical errors but, if the document is otherwise intelligible, such shortcomings may be overlooked. In a case where the notary feels constrained to obtain an English language translation of a foreign language document, he or she may request the translator to verify the translation on affidavit or by statutory declaration. Precedents of such an affidavit and declaration are contained in Appendix 3 and 3A respectively to the supplement.

Acknowledgement Letter
In recent times, coinciding with the unprecedented growth in overseas property acquisitions by Irish citizens, many Irish notaries were

voicing concern regarding the form and content of some foreign powers of attorney being furnished for execution by Irish citizens. The Faculty of Notaries Public in Ireland appointed a special committee to examine the matter. The committee found that the concerns were justified. A standard form of acknowledgement letter was produced by the Faculty to address the concerns that had been expressed.

The acknowledgement letter spells out in unambiguous language the relationship between the appearer and the notary public whose services he or she requires. In summary the appearer formally acknowledges that he or she fully understands the nature and purpose of the power of attorney; that it has been explained to the appearer by a person in whom the appearer has trust; that the notary is not his or her legal adviser or the author of the foreign power of attorney which is to be signed and notarised; that the notary has told the appearer that he or she (the notary) is not competent in the foreign language in which the power of attorney is written and is not qualified in the laws of the country in which the power of attorney is to operate; that powers of attorney are important legal documents which can have serious consequences for persons giving them, and that it is important that the appearer should obtain competent advice as to the legal, financial and taxation implications of the transaction generally. The text of an acknowledgement letter in the singular and plural forms will be found in Appendix 4 and Appendix 5 to this supplement. It is recommended that all notaries keep a small supply of acknowledgement letters, in both forms, in readiness for the day on which such a document will be required.

The Faculty has further recommended that notaries obtain a rubber stamp which can be applied to all foreign language documents produced to the notary for attestation, stating that the notarial act applied to the foreign language document extends only to verification of the identity and legal capacity of the appearer and the due execution of the document, unless otherwise expressly stated in the English language. A specimen of such stamp is contained in Chapter 6 (Notarial Accoutrements) of this supplement.

Attestations in absentia

In the principal work, notaries were cautioned against completing an attestation to a document that had not been executed in the notary's presence. That caution is now repeated in the light of the publicity generated in the media to such an occurrence in a neighbouring jurisdiction. In the case in question, a power of attorney, prepared in connection with a divorce settlement involving foreign property, was left at the notary's office in his absence for the purpose of having the divorced wife's signature witnessed and notarised. The notary, on his return to his office, purported to attest the signature (already subscribed) as a notarial act and returned the document to the foreign lawyers dealing with the matter. The divorced wife subsequently denied having executed the document. The matter was referred to a statutory tribunal exercising jurisdiction over notaries public. The tribunal found that, by purporting to attest a document that had not been signed in his actual presence, the notary had failed to establish the true identity of the signatory or her understanding of the document as proper notarial practice demanded. The notary was found guilty of misconduct and fined £1,000. The case was widely reported and the notary named in national and local newspapers and professional journals.

Presentation of Documents to Notary: Unbound Pages

Notaries are cautioned against attesting a signature, or providing a notarial certificate, on unbound papers i.e. a document consisting of a number of loose pages. A notary who does so may unwittingly present an opportunity for additional pages to be subsequently included or for new pages, with altered text, to be substituted for existing pages. Accordingly, where the document presented to the notary consists of several loose pages, the notary, having completed his or her notarial act, should inform the appearer that the notary is obliged to bind the pages together and proceed to do so. A notary who is presented with a multipage document, the pages of which are held together with a staple or a treasury tag, should secure the pages together using either eyelets and tape or stitching thread (as was formerly done with deeds) or cover the staple or tag with a deposit of sealing wax or an adhesive seal to which the notary's stamp is applied in such a way as to render obvious any attempt to separate the pages or remove the seal. In dealing with a multipage document the notary should have an official stamp, containing the notary's name or initials, that can be neatly applied to each page of the document (excluding the signature page) thus providing an assurance to the person relying on the document that no substitution of pages could have occurred. A specimen of such a stamp is contained in Chapter 6 (Notarial Accoutrements) of this supplement.

Notarial certificates should, where possible, be typed on a separate page to be annexed to the document being notarised rather than on the document itself. The notary's signature verifies the due execution of the document with reference to which it is subscribed or on which it appears and not the contents of the document. Likewise, verifying stamps (or seals) should not be applied to the face of documents purporting to be testamurs of degrees, diplomas or other qualifications. Preferably, such stamp (or seal) should be applied on a separate sheet of paper to be attached to the testamur. Because a notary can never be certain that the document purporting to evidence a degree, diploma or other qualification produced to him or her is the original document and not a facsimile or a forgery, it is suggested that the notary, for his or her protection, should prepare a notarial act on the lines of the precedent in Appendix 6 to the supplement.

Notarial Fees

In the matter of fees, there are no prescribed, recommended or set fees for notarial work and it would be contrary to competition law for the Faculty, or any group of notaries public, to determine or recommend a scale of fees for such work. Section 4(1) of the Competition Act, 2002 prohibits and renders void 'all agreements between undertakings, decisions by association of undertakings and concerted practices which have as their object or effect the prevention, restriction or distortion of competition in trade in any goods or services in the State or in any part of the State'. Price fixing for services is specifically prohibited. In any event, the circumstances of each case will differ as regards the nature and amount of the work involved and the time needed for its completion. If the service entails travel, mileage may become an extra feature of the notary's charges. The Faculty, however, has advocated to its members that notarial fees should never be disproportionate or exorbitant but should reasonably reflect the true cost of the service provided, based on the amount of skill and time involved and responsibility undertaken. The Faculty has also recommended that sympathetic treatment be given to cases involving human tragedy or emotional distress.

Chapter 6

NOTARIAL ACCOUTREMENTS
FORMS OF CERTIFICATION

In Chapter 6 of the principal work, and elsewhere in this supplement, reference is made to certain stamps that a notary public should have readily available for various verifications he or she is asked to carry out. One such stamp is for certifying documents to be true copies. The older form of this stamp would have read as follows:

'I hereby certify that the within document is a true copy of the original with which it has been compared while in my possession.'

In recent years there has been much debate regarding the appropriate wording for such a stamp. It is argued that, unless the notary is the author of the original document, the copy of which he or she is asked to certify, or was present at its execution, he or she will seldom be in a position to assert that the document produced to him or her as an original is in fact that. It may be the original in one instance, but on another occasion it may be a facsimile. In yet another instance, the document may be counterfeit. The notary must, therefore, be careful not to assume responsibility for matters outside his or her actual knowledge. Furthermore, it has recently become the practice of certain countries to require the notarial certification of a copy document to describe the nature of the original document. It is considered that a stamp for certifying copy documents along the following lines would meet such situations:

'I hereby certify that the within document is a true copy of the document produced to me and described as _____
(e.g. power of attorney, deed poll, passport) with which it has been compared while in my possession.'

In Chapter 5 of this supplement, reference is made to a stamp to be applied by a notary public to a document written in a foreign language (or partly in a foreign language and partly in the English language) the execution of which the notary has attested and, or, has notarised. Such a stamp should contain the following words:

'The notarial act applied to the within document extends only to verification of the identity and legal capacity of the appearer(s) and the due execution of the document unless otherwise expressly stated in the English language.'

An acknowledgment of the appearer's understanding of the nature and purpose of the document might also be usefully included.

Reference was also made in Chapter 5 to a stamp that may be used to identify and authenticate individual pages of a multipage document. A specimen of such a stamp is printed below. Additional details can be inserted in the stamp as appropriate.

Notaries are frequently asked by Solicitors to certify copies of birth certificates, death certificates and marriage certificates as true copies. For this purpose, the notary is usually furnished with the official certificate and a photocopy. When compiling the wording of such a certificate, it should be remembered that the official document issued by or on behalf of the Registrar of Births, Deaths and Marriages, though loosely referred to as an original document, is itself a certificate compiled from entries made in the relevant registers in the custody of the Ard Chláraitheoir (Chief Registrar) or the District Registrar. Certification in words such as 'certified a true copy' followed by the notary's signature and stamp is inadequate and would not generally be acceptable internationally. The following form of certificate to be applied on the back of the copy official certificate is suggested:

'I hereby certify that the document on the reverse hereof is a true copy of the official [Birth Certificate] [Death Certificate] [Marriage Certificate][1] purporting to have been issued by the _____[2] at _____[3] on _____[4] with which said copy has been compared while in my possession.'

Notaries will have found in the course of their practice that many foreign documents received in the State for execution do not end with the formal testimonium (In witness whereof) and attestation (signed and sealed etc.) clauses with which common law practitioners will be familiar. Consequently, there may appear to be no nexus or sequence between the body of the document and the appearer's execution of the document, or between the appearer's signature on the document and the notarial act. To deal with such situations, it is recommended that notaries either type in an attestation or equip themselves with a stamp substantially in the following form:

'Signed before me by the above named
at
on this   day of   200

Notary Public'

If the document is written in a foreign language, it may be appropriate to translate the words 'Signed before me' into the foreign language. For example, if the document is in French, the words 'Signe pardevant moi' would be appropriate; if in Italian, the words 'Sottoscrito innanzi a me'; if in Spanish, the words 'Firmado ante mi'; if in Portuguese, the words 'Assignado per ante mim' and if in German, the words 'Unter dach vor mir' to be followed, in each case, by the notary's signature, place of attestation and the date.

Notes:
[1] Delete as appropriate
[2] Insert Registrar or Superintendent Registrar, as the case may be
[3] Insert place of issue
[4] Insert date of issue

Seals, signs and signs-manual

In the principal work, reference is made to the notary's official seal, its design and content. It is further explained in a footnote dealing with the seal (L. sigillum) that in earlier times a seal, impressed on a deposit of wax, might have been the only form of execution or attestation appearing on a document. In the middle ages it became the practice for a notary to affix a sign (L. signum) by hand to the document being executed, usually in addition to the seal. Such signs or signs-manual, from which developed the modern signature, were frequently individualistic and personalised in form and were often preceded by the words '*signoque meo solito et assueto signavi*', meaning that the document was executed with the notary's usual and customary sign. For example, a notary whose surname was Kidd, adopted a goat's head as the centerpiece of his sign-manual. Notaries also embellished their signs-manual by adding mottoes, paraphs and rubrics to them. A notary whose name was Lucas incorporated the words '*ex tenebras lux*' as a motto in his sign-manual. The purpose of these additions was to make the notary's sign not only unique but difficult to imitate. Forgery is not a recently developed art. Sadly for those notaries with an artistic flare, the signs-manual with their flourishes and mottoes have been replaced in modern times with the signature, rubber stamp and the metal embossing seal. However, the one thing to remain constant is the obligation on the part of the notary to keep his or her stamp and seal in a secure place at all times. Illustrations of signs-manual with paraphs and mottoes are depicted below.

The Irish Notary

Illustrations of Notarial Marks i.e., Signs-manual, Paraphs and Rubrics in use in the 14th to 16th centuries.

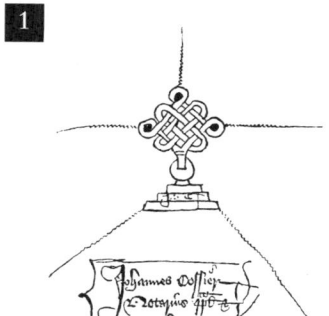

Notarial Mark of John Cossier, 1390.

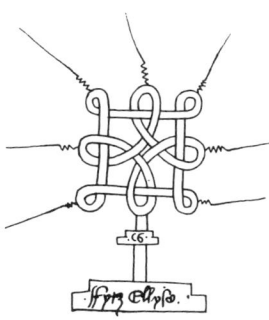

The sign of William Fytz Ellyse diocese of Ossory, public notary by apostolic authority, 1448.

Notarial Mark of William Slade, 1465.

Notarial Rubric of William Slade, 1465.

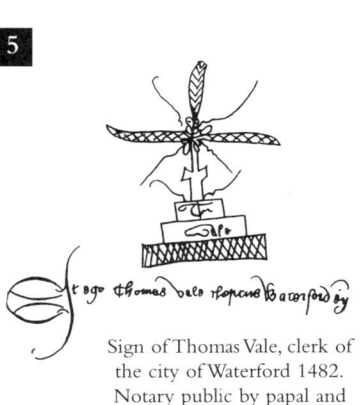

Sign of Thomas Vale, clerk of the city of Waterford 1482. Notary public by papal and imperial authorities.

Notarial Mark of Thomas Lucas, 1580.

Chapter 7

OATHS: SUBSTANCE, FORM AND PROCEDURE

Statutory Declarations

It was explained in Chapter 7 of the principal work that a person empowered under the Statutory Declarations Act, 1938 (No. 37 of 1938) to take and receive statutory declarations e.g. notary public, commissioner for oaths or peace commissioner, must state in the attestation to the statutory declaration that the declarant is personally known to him or her, or has been identified to him or her by a person personally known to him or her. In other words personal identification had to be established before taking the declaration. In recent years, due to the unprecedented growth in the numbers of foreign nationals in Ireland, an unforeseen difficulty has arisen for notaries and others authorised and empowered to take and receive statutory declarations. The difficulty arises due to the notary's inability to establish identification based on his or her personal knowledge of the declarant. In such circumstances the intended declarant may have to be turned away.

The Faculty of Notaries Public in Ireland made representations to the Minister for Justice, Equality and Law Reform seeking to have the problem addressed by legislation. The Minister and the Department responded positively and it is satisfactory to be able to report at this juncture that provision is contained in Part 7 of the Civil Law (Miscellaneous Provisions) Bill, 2006 (No. 20 of 2006) aimed at addressing the position. Section 59 (1) of the Bill, if enacted in its present form, will amend section 2 of the Statutory Declarations Act, 1938 by substituting a new text as subsection (2), enlarging the existing provision. While the proposed new subsection restates the requirement for personal identification, it offers other means of establishing identity where personal identification cannot be provided. In the latter situation, the person taking the statutory declaration may establish identity by reference to a 'relevant document' (described in section 2, subsection (4) of the Bill) containing a photograph of the declarant. Relevant document for this purpose means:

(a) a valid passport issued by or on behalf of an authority recognised by the Government,

(b) a national identity card issued by the authorities of -
  (i) a Member State of the European Union,
  (ii) the Swiss Confederation, or
  (iii) a Contracting Party to the EEA Agreement,

(c) a document which is equivalent to a passport, issued by or on behalf of an authority recognised by the Government, which establishes the identity and nationality of the person to whom the document relates.

(d) a travel document issued by the Minister for Justice, Equality and Law Reform under section 4 of the Refugee Act, 1996, or

(e) a travel document other than a document to which paragraph *(d)* refers issued by the State solely for the purpose of providing the holder with a document which can serve in lieu of a national passport.

'EEA Agreement' above means the Agreement on the European Economic Area signed at Oporto on 2 May 1992 as amended for the time being.

It will be noted that a driving licence is not included as a relevant document. This, it appears, is due to the fact that thousands of spurious driving licences are in use throughout the world, thus rendering the driving licence an unreliable document for the purpose of establishing identity. A driving licence may, however, be accepted as evidence of identification in minor domestic transactions, but not when a statutory declaration is required. Notaries should be aware that the form of statutory declaration (including the attestation) is set forth in the Bill. For ease of reference, the form of Statutory Declaration is contained in Appendix 8 to the supplement. A declaration that departs from that form may not have the benefits given to a statutory declaration. Indeed it may not be a statutory declaration if the departure is significant.

The ePassport

In early 2006, the Minister for Foreign Affairs, Mr. Dermot C. Ahern, T.D. announced the proposed introduction of a new form of Irish passport described as a biometric passport. Commencing 16 October 2006 the new style passport, referred to now as the 'ePassport', is being issued by the Department of Foreign Affairs

(Passport Office) on a phased basis. This passport bears on the front cover the words 'Pas' and 'Passport' together with a gold international ePassport symbol indicating that the passport is electronically readable. It also instantly distinguishes the new passport from the older form of passport while the latter remains in use. Existing passports can continue to be used for all purposes until they reach the expiry date on the data page. The ePassport differs from the pre October 2006 passport in that, in addition to the photographic facial image of the passport holder on the data page, it carries the facial image and other details of the passport holder in digitised form. This information is securely stored in a microchip embedded in the data page of the ePassport. The digitised image and other personal details of the passport holder are not capable of being viewed with the naked eye and may only be read with an electronic reader available to officials at border controls. Whether the passport is in the old or new form the notary will, as heretofore, concern himself or herself with the photographic facial image and printed personal details on the passport data page.

Administering Oaths etc.

For the convenience of notaries public, forms of words to be spoken by deponents and declarants when swearing affidavits, making affirmations and statutory declarations are set forth below:

Affidavits

'I swear by Almighty God that this is my true name and handwriting; that the signature subscribed hereto is my usual signature; that I have read the affidavit and the contents are true.'

Affirmations

'I solemnly and sincerely affirm that this is my true name and handwriting; that the signature subscribed hereto is my usual signature; that I have read the affirmation and the contents are true.'

Statutory Declarations

'I solemnly and sincerely declare that this is my true name and handwriting; that the signature subscribed hereto is my usual signature; that I have read the declaration and the contents are true.'

Where the deponent or declarant is unable to read, the words 'that the affidavit/affirmation/declaration has been read over to me by A.B. notary public' should be substituted for the words 'That I have read' etc.

In the principal work it is recommended that notaries keep a copy of the Koran (Qur'an) for use on those occasions when it is required to administer an oath to a person professing the Islamic religion. However, in a recent international publication on notarial practice it was suggested that to ask a Muslim to swear on the Qur'an, whether or not involving touching the Holy Book, may be considered offensive on the grounds that, for the Muslim, the efficacy of the oath lies in the invocation of Allah and not in the act of holding or touching the Qur'an. In a letter to the Dean of the Faculty of Notaries Public in Ireland dated 29 August, 2006 the Imam of the Islamic Cultural Centre of Ireland, Sheikh Hussein Halawa, stated that, as a Muslim religious authority, he did not perceive the practice described in the principal work as contradicting Islamic teachings. Notaries should always be sensitive to religious difference when administering oaths and should never require a person to take an oath in a form that would be offensive to deponents' religious beliefs.

Companies Acts – Foreign Statutory Declarations

Section 6 of the Investment Funds, Companies and Miscellaneous Provisions Act 2006 (No. 41 of 2006) contains provisions for the making and receiving outside the State of statutory declarations in compliance with or for the purposes of the Companies Acts 1963 to 2006 and regularises certain statutory declarations made outside the State before the passing of the Act otherwise than in accordance with the Diplomatic and Consular Officers (Provision of Services) Act, 1993.

Chapter 8

STRUCTURE OF CERTAIN LEGAL DOCUMENTS

Powers of Attorney

In Chapter 8 of the principal work reference is made, *inter alia*, to the legal instrument known as a power of attorney and to the law and practice governing such instruments. In 1996, the existing law was substantially amended and updated under the provisions of the Powers of Attorney Act, 1996 (in this chapter referred to as 'the 1996 Act'), which additionally introduced a new legal instrument known as an Enduring Power of Attorney ('EPA'). This latter instrument will be fully considered later in this chapter.

Pursuant to section 2 of the 1996 Act, a power of attorney is defined as meaning:

> 'an instrument signed by or by direction of a person (the donor) or a provision contained in such an instrument, giving the donee the power to act on behalf of the donor in accordance with the terms of the instrument.'

Prior to the enactment of the 1996 Act, there were no special provisions governing the creation of a power of attorney. Powers of attorney generally, until the enactment of the 1996 Act, were governed by the common law and provisions of the Conveyancing Acts, 1881 and 1882. Some provisions of these Acts were repealed by the 1996 Act.

Section 15 of the 1996 Act provides that where a power of attorney is signed at the direction of the donor, it shall be signed in the presence of the donor and of another person who shall attest the instrument as witness. This would appear to govern a situation where the donor, though otherwise legally competent, is physically incapable of signing the instrument.

Section 15(2) of the 1996 Act provides that a power of attorney is not required to be made under seal, but this statutory provision is stated to be without prejudice to any other requirement in or under any other enactment as to the witnessing of powers of attorney or as to the execution of such instruments by bodies corporate.

The General Power of Attorney

Uniquely, in the 1996 Act, the form of a general power of attorney is set out in the third schedule. The form is not prescribed to be, in an absolute sense, a mandatory requirement which would render a power of attorney invalid if not followed. Under section 16 of the 1996 Act a general power of attorney in the form contained in the third schedule to the Act shall 'operate to confer on the donee or donees of the power, acting in accordance with its terms, authority to do on behalf of the donor, anything which the donor can lawfully do by attorney'.

The form of a general power of attorney contained in the third schedule of the 1996 Act is set out here:

'THIS GENERAL POWER OF ATTORNEY is made this
day of   200
by AB of
I appoint CD of
[or CD of   and EF of
jointly (or jointly and severally)] to be my attorney[s] in accordance with section 16 of the Powers of Attorney Act, 1996.
IN WITNESS etc.'

In effect, this form of wording gives notaries and other legal practitioners a very simple form of a general power of attorney. However, section 16(2) of the 1996 Act provides that the above form of a general power of attorney does not apply to functions the donor has as a trustee or personal representative, or as a tenant for life within the meaning of the Settled Land Act, 1882, or as trustee or other person exercising the powers of a tenant for life under section 60 of the Settled Land Act, 1882. The death or incapacity of the donor usually revokes the power.

Section 17 of the 1996 Act is also of some legal significance for notaries. Firstly, section 17(1) re-enacts section 46 of the Conveyancing Act, 1881 which authorised a donee of a power of attorney to execute any instrument with his or her own signature and, where sealing is required, with his or her own seal, and to do any other thing in his or her name, by the authority of the donor of the power. Any instrument executed or thing done in that manner shall be as effective as if executed or done by the donee with the signature and seal, or, as the case may be, in the name of the donor of the power.

Section 17(2) of the 1996 Act provides that where a power of attorney is being exercised on behalf of a corporation to convey any estate or interest in property in the name of or on behalf of the corporation sole or aggregate, the donee may execute a conveyance by signing his or her name as acting in the name or on behalf of the corporation in the presence of at least one witness and, in the case of a deed, by affixing his or her own seal. A corporation sole consists of one person and his successors; a corporation aggregate consists of more than one member e.g. a company registered under the Companies Acts which must have at least two members, although one may be the nominee of the other.

Brian Gallagher in his annotation to The Powers of Attorney Act, 1996, (Round Hall, Sweet & Maxwell) states that the best practice in relation to the execution of deeds by the donee of a power of attorney is as follows:

'1. The deed is prepared in the name of the donor;
2. The attestation clause states that the deed is executed on behalf of the donor by the attorney;
3. The donee executes by writing in his or her own hand 'AB (the donor) by his or her attorney CD (the donee)' who then signs his or her own name.'

Where the corporation aggregate is authorised under a power of attorney to convey any interest in property in the name or on behalf of any other person (including another body corporate), a person appointed for that purpose by the corporation may execute the deed or other instrument in the name of such other person (including such other body corporate); and where an instrument appears to be executed by a person so appointed, then in favour of a purchaser, the instrument is deemed to have been executed by that person unless the contrary is shown.

Section 18 of the 1996 Act replaces sections 8 and 9 of the Conveyancing Act, 1882 and deals essentially with the protection of the donee of a power of attorney and third parties where the power is revoked. Section 18(1) provides that a donee of a power of attorney who acts in pursuance of the power at a time when it has been revoked shall not, by reason of the revocation, incur any liability (either to the donor or to any other person) if, at that time, the donee did not know that the power had been revoked. The reader is referred to other detailed provisions in section 18 of the 1996 Act.

Section 19 of the 1996 Act confers specific protection on the transferee of registered securities which are transferred by the donee of a power of attorney for the purposes of a stock exchange transaction.

In relation to powers of attorney given for security, section 20 of the 1996 Act provides that where the power of attorney is expressed to be irrevocable and is given to secure:

(a) a proprietary interest of the donee of the power; or
(b) the performance of an obligation owed to the donee,

then, so long as the donee has that interest or the obligation remains undischarged, the power shall not be revoked:

(a) by the donor without the consent of the donee; or
(b) by the death, incapacity, or bankruptcy of the donor; or if the donor is a body corporate, by its winding-up or dissolution.

This section was amended by section 5 of the Family Law (Miscellaneous Provisions) Act, 1997.

In the context of proof of an instrument creating a power of attorney, section 21 of the 1996 Act introduces a new method of proving powers of attorney. Previously the matter was governed by section 48(4) of the Conveyancing Act, 1881, which was repealed by the 1996 Act. Section 21 of the 1996 Act provides that a power of attorney may be proved by the production of an original instrument or copy certified by the donor, or by a solicitor, or member firm (within the meaning of the Stock Exchange Act, 1995) or in such other manner as the court approves. Alternatively, where the instrument has been deposited in the Central Office of the High Court pursuant to section 22 of the 1996 Act, the instrument may be proved by a copy attested in accordance with that section. Section 22 of the 1996 Act provides that an instrument creating a power of attorney, its execution being verified by affidavit, statutory declaration or other sufficient evidence, may, with the affidavit or declaration, if any, be deposited in the Central Office of the High Court. It appears that section 22 is not mandatory and powers of attorney do not have to be deposited in the Central Office of the High Court to be valid.

In the context of a purchaser of any estate or interest in land, section 23 of the 1996 Act provides that a purchaser of any estate or interest in land is entitled to have any instrument creating a power of attorney which affects title thereto, or a certified copy or an attested copy thereof, furnished by the vendor to the purchaser free of expense.

Enduring Powers of Attorney: Meaning and Purpose

In the principal work (1987), reference was made to an instrument then available under English law for use in England and Wales and described as an Enduring Power of Attorney ('EPA'). A similar instrument was introduced into Irish law by the Powers of Attorney Act, 1996 as amended by the Family Law (Divorce) Act, 1996 and the Family Law (Miscellaneous Provisions) Act, 1997, (in this chapter described as 'the 1996 Act').

The preliminary recital to the 1996 Act describes the Act as providing 'for powers of attorney to operate when the donor of the power is or is becoming mentally incapable and to amend in other respects the law relating to powers of attorney generally'. The problem with the commonly understood power of attorney, whether general or special in form, is that it ceases to have effect when the donor becomes mentally incapable. The principal features of an EPA are set out in the following paragraphs.

Section 5 of the 1996 Act sets out the essence of an EPA, which is that the donor intends the power to be effective during his or her subsequent mental incapacity, if that is to occur. The Minister for Justice, Equality and Law Reform was authorised to make regulations in relation to certain matters concerning EPAs. These regulations, Enduring Powers of Attorney Regulations, 1996 (S.I. No. 196 of 1996) and Enduring Powers of Attorney (Personal Care Decisions) Regulations, 1996 (S.I. No. 287 of 1996) provide for the form and manner of execution of an EPA. However, section 10(5)(a) of the 1996 Act provides that an EPA shall be treated as sufficient in point of form and expression if it differs in an immaterial respect from the form prescribed by the regulations. The regulations contain an explanatory memorandum which forms part of the EPA to ensure that the EPA incorporates adequate information as to the effect of creating or accepting the power.

Four classes of Person to Execute EPA

The EPA must be executed by four classes of persons: the donor, a solicitor, a registered medical practitioner, and the attorney. A registered medical practitioner must make a statement that in his or her opinion at the time the document was executed, the donor had mental capacity. The regulations provide that an attorney 'shall keep adequate accounts of the management' of the property and affairs of the donor and, 'in particular, of any expenditure to meet the needs of persons other than the donor or to make any gifts authorised by the enduring power'.

The regulations also state that the EPA 'may make provision in relation to the remuneration of an attorney'. If no such provision is made, the attorney can only recover out of pocket expenses.

Notice of Execution of EPA

Furthermore, the regulations i.e. the statutory instruments specified above, provide that notice of the execution of an EPA by the donor shall be given by or on behalf of the donor to at least two persons named by the donor in the EPA. None of them shall be an attorney under the power. At least one of them must be:

    (i) the donor's spouse, if living with the donor; or
    (ii) if clause (i) does not apply (if the donor is unmarried, widowed or separated), a child of the donor; or

(iii) if clauses (i) and (ii) do not apply, a relative, (i.e. parent, sibling, grandchild, widow, widower of a child, nephew or niece (if any)), of the donor.

The form of notice of the execution of an EPA is set out in the regulations, specified above.

Registration of Enduring Power of Attorney

A Practice Direction entitled Powers of Attorney Act, 1996: Enduring Powers of Attorney Regulations, 1996 (S.I. No. 196 of 1996) deals with the registration of an EPA in the High Court. This is to be done by means of special summons to be issued in the Central Office of the High Court. The special summons is to be addressed to the Registrar of Wards of Court. The practice direction states that the application to the Registrar of Wards of Court must be grounded on an affidavit which should contain certain information set out in the practice direction and should exhibit the documents as specified in the practice direction. As soon as practicable after the issue of the special summons, two copies of the special summons and of the affidavit grounding it and copies of the exhibits (certified by the applicant's solicitor as being true copies) should be delivered to the office of the Registrar of Wards of Court. The effect of registration of an EPA is that no revocation of the power by the donor shall be valid unless and until the court confirms the revocation under the 1996 Act.

The High Court has certain functions in respect of a registered EPA and the court shall on application to it by the donor, the attorney or any other interested party, as the case may be, determine any question as to the meaning or effect of the registered EPA.

Reference may be made here to the very useful booklet, *Enduring Powers of Attorney: Guidelines for Solicitors*, issued by the Probate, Administration and Taxation Committee of the Law Society of Ireland in April 2004.

Northern Ireland

The position in Northern Ireland in relation to an EPA is much the same as in this jurisdiction (which is described above) and as respects Northern Ireland, reference may be made to the Enduring Powers of Attorney (Northern Ireland) Order, 1987 (S.I. No. 1627 of 1987) (N.I. 16) and the Enduring Powers of Attorney (Northern Ireland Consequential Amendment) Order, 1987 (S.I. 1628 of 1987).

Chapter 9

SHIPS PROTESTS

Ireland, being a maritime nation with major ports around its coastline, cannot but be involved with ships and matters that concern them. Damage to a vessel or its cargo are always matters of concern to shipowners, their insurers and those whose job it is to navigate them. It is in this area of shipping that the notary public is most likely to become involved when he or she is called upon to receive and make a ship protest. The ship protest is a relic of the law merchant.

In the principal work, a ship protest, frequently referred to as a 'ship's protest', is described as a statement made in solemn form by the master or other officer of a ship, in the presence of a notary public, concerning an event or happening at sea arising from damage which is feared to have occurred to the ship, its cargo or crew. The facts declared before the notary are recorded in writing by the notary and signed by the master of the vessel or other ship's officer making the statement. Precedents of a note of protest and a protest are contained in appendices 47 to 50 of the principal work. A ship protest is concerned with fact and not opinion. Consequently, while a master may fear damage to the ship or cargo because of some occurrence at sea e.g. force 10 gale causing the vessel to roll and cargo to shift on board, it is the occurrence giving rise to such fear that is the fact to be recorded.

As there is no statutory or prescribed form for a ship protest, it may take the form of a sworn statement, statutory declaration or a formal act signed and sealed by the notary. A copy of the protest is then entered in the notary's protocol book or register, dated and signed. Notaries who undertake such work usually have their own forms and precedents, often handed down from generation to generation. The late Dean of the Faculty of Notaries Public in Ireland, James Donegan of Cobh, a notary, solicitor and sailor was one such notary. Unquestionably, the most knowledgeable of Irish notaries in maritime matters, the ship protest was his most favoured notarial commission.

The precedents of a Note of Entry of the Ship or Vessel (Note of Protest) and of a Statement of Sea Protest (Ship Protest) at the end of this chapter were kindly provided by the Donegan family from the records of the late James Donegan. It will be noted that the description 'Sea Protest', corresponding to the Spanish 'Protesta de Mare', is used in these precedents in lieu of the more common description 'Ship Protest' as if to enforce the notion that though the ship, through its master, may be the protestor, the protest is against the sea which, in one capricious moment, may wreak havoc on a ship, its cargo and crew.

Note of Protest

A ship protest must be made at the earliest opportunity, ideally within 24 hours of the vessel arriving in port. Any apparent delay must be accounted for. The protest may be made on the vessel, in a shipping agent's office or in the notary's office, depending on the circumstances. Because of the time required, the inconvenience of the location or the exigencies of the case, and because notaries do not carry a stock of forms suitable for all occasions, it is now almost the universal practice for the notary, in the first instance, to prepare a 'note of protest' instead of a full protest. The note of protest is a form of preliminary notice given to all concerned by the master or other officer of a ship of an event or happening affecting the ship, its cargo or crew about which he intends to make a fuller statement at some future time should the need arise. The same essential details will be given in the note of protest, albeit in shorter form, as will be provided, with more elaboration, in the full protest. The efficacy of the note of protest derives from the fact that it is made in the presence of a notary public whose credit and standing is unquestioned among civilised nations and that it is formally registered in the notary's Ships Protest Register.

Extended Protest

Should a full ship protest (as distinct from a note of protest) be requested by the master, ship owner or insurer subsequent to the entry of a note of protest, the notary will prepare such document based on the facts previously recorded. It may be elaborated by incorporating relevant entries from the ship's log. In certain circumstances the master of vessel may desire other ship's officers to join in his protest in order to corroborate his statement. This may be done by way of an addendum to the master's note of protest or in a separate document. In either event, the protest, described as an 'extended protest', will be signed by the ship's officer or officers making it and then signed and sealed by the notary public.

Requisites for a Ship Protest

A notary public on being requested by a shipping agent to meet a vessel at portside for the purpose of taking a ship protest should prepare himself or herself for such commission by requesting the following information in advance:

1. The name, description and place of registration of the vessel;
2. The name and address of the owner or charterer of the vessel;
3. The name(s) and title(s) of the person(s) intending to make the protest;
4. The port from which the vessel sailed immediately before the occurrence;
5. The port at which it was intended the ship should first berth;
6. The port at which the vessel will be berthed at the time of making the protest;
7. The general nature of the cargo;
8. The occurrence which has given rise to the need for the protest and the date or dates and times over which the occurrence(s) extended.

Before commencing the ship protest, the notary should request proof of identity of the master or ship's officer by reference to his passport and inspection of his official papers i.e. his licence and ticket, in order to establish his rank, qualifications or status.

The notary should then inspect the ship's papers which, under international law, are required to be carried. The notary must also inspect the ship's log in order to compare the entries recorded in it with the narrative which will be given in the protest. For additional forms and precedents, the reader is referred to the appendices to the principal work.

NOTE OF ENTRY OF SHIP OR VESSEL IN THE PROTEST REGISTER

On the ……… day of ………………, in the Year of Our Lord Two Thousand and …….. at the Office of me, J.D., Notary Public, in and for the City of Cork and the Port of Cork, personally appeared, Captain E.F. of the Vessel the M.V. '……………..' of the Port of ……………… and of the burthen per register measurement ….. tons, which sailed on a Voyage from …………… to …………… on the …… day of ……………… 200 and arrived at Cork on the ………… day of ………………… 200 laden with a cargo of …………… And the said Captain E.F. hereby gives Notice of his intention of Protesting for general protection and causes this note or minute of all and singular the premises to be entered in this Registry: 'encountered very heavy seas on voyage, ship straining, rolling and pitching heavily, shipping water over all and I fear damage to ship and/or cargo.'

EF	J.D.
Captain	Notary Public

STATEMENT OF SEA PROTEST

Port of _____
To: Notary/Consul
The day of 200

I, E.F. Master of the vessel the M.V. '…………………' of the Port of …………… Official No. ……………. of the burthen per register measurement of …….. tons or thereabouts ………….. which sailed from the Port of ……………. on the …… day of ………. 200 with a cargo of ………., bound for the Port of ………………….. and arrived at the Port of Cork on the …… day of

…………… 200 fearing, notwithstanding all measures of good seamanship taken by me and my crew, that some loss or damage might have been caused to the said Ship or her appurtenances or cargo or some other property on board by reason that during the voyage the vessel met with some stormy weather and heavy seas, the ship suffered rolling and pitching heavily shipping water fore and aft and spraying overall, hatches and vents being continually awash, the vessel, to avoid the risk of any or any further damage or injury to ship, cargo or crew, was caused to reduce engine speed and change her course taking shelter on the road for protection from the stormy weather. Hereby, I declare Sea Protest against any claims by all persons or person whom it shall or may concern, and declare that all and every damage and loss sustained by the said ship and/or cargo, or some other property on board, in consequence of the events aforesaid, are and shall be borne by those who, according to the laws and customs of the sea shall bear the consequences thereof, the same having occurred as above-stated not by or through the want of care of myself or my crew. Before declaring the Sea Protest the cargo holds were not opened. I hereby reserve the right to extend the same Sea Protest at time and place convenient.

E.F.
Master

Before me J.D. Notary Public

EXTRACTS FROM THE LOG BOOK NO. OF THE M.V. '…………………..'
[Given as an example]

21.10	12.48	Weather forecast received 'In the East part of the English Channel expect wind SW-10'. Permission to drop anchor at …………. received from the ……………. Coast Guard.
21.10	13.28	Dropped anchor at ……………………………..

23.10	00.15	Picked up anchor. The vessel is under way. Proceed to port of destination ....
23.10	12.00	The ship pitching and rolling heavily from the sea swell and waves. The hatches continually washed by seawater.
23.10	18.03	The hatches continually washed by seawater. The vessel following the optimal course to swell.
23.10	24.00	The hatches continually washed by seawater.

Chapter 10

BILLS OF EXCHANGE

It was stated in the principal work that the noting and protesting of bills of exchange and promissory notes for non-acceptance or non-payment formed a substantial part of the work of a notary public. In the two decades that have passed since that work was published this aspect of banking and commerce has undergone a dramatic change. Though trade bills i.e. bills of exchange and promissory notes used by exporters to secure payment for goods supplied on credit terms, are still in use, they have been replaced to a large extent by more modern and efficient banking and commercial instruments including documentary credits; and paper-based payment instruments have been largely replaced with electronic collection and payment systems. However, for as long as bills of exchange continue to be used in foreign trade, the notary public must maintain his or her knowledge of the law and practice relating to such instruments.

At page 121 of the principal work it was mentioned that the practice of adding days of grace when determining the time of payment of bills of exchange (not payable on demand) continued in the Republic of Ireland after the practice had been abolished in the United Kingdom under the Banking and Financial Dealings Act, 1971. Days of grace were three extra days added in accordance with section 14 of the Bills of Exchange Act, 1882 to the time of payment as fixed by the bill. The bill then became payable on the last of such added days. Other provisions dealt with the situation where the last day of grace fell on a Sunday, Christmas Day or Good Friday or otherwise fell on a day that was a bank holiday under the Bank Holidays Act, 1871. In 1989, days of grace were abolished in the Republic of Ireland by section 132 (1) (b) of the Central Bank Act, 1989 which replaced paragraph (1) of section 14 of the Bills of Exchange Act, 1882 with the following new text:

'(1) The bill is due and payable in all cases on the last day of the time of payment as fixed by the bill or, if that is a non-business day, on the succeeding business day:

Provided that nothing in this paragraph shall operate to prevent a bill being paid by the drawee on a Saturday (other than a Saturday that is a public holiday or to which paragraph (d) of the definition of 'non-business days' in section 2 of this Act relates) or cause him to incur any liability thereby, where -
(a) the drawee is a banker, and
(b) the Saturday concerned is the last day fixed by the bill as the time of payment, and
(c) the drawee is normally open for business on a Saturday at his address given in or ascertainable from the bill,
and, accordingly, presentation and payment of such a bill on the Saturday shall be valid and shall discharge it as fully as if it had been presented and paid on the next succeeding business day: but this provision shall not be construed as compelling the person entitled to payment on the bill to accept such payment on the Saturday.'

The Central Bank Act, 1989 made other changes to the Bills of Exchange Act and to the Cheques Act, 1959 but these changes do not impact on the work of the notary public in relation to foreign bills.

Chapter 11

LEGALISATION AND THE APOSTILLE

Ireland has been a permanent member of the Hague Conference on Private International Law since its foundation in 1955. This intergovernmental organisation, which has its seat at The Hague, has as its objective the progressive unification of the rules of private international law. Agreements concluded as a result of the deliberations of the Conference are recorded by means of Conventions. Such Conventions are either signed by participating States on their being done or concluded, or are left open to them for signature and ratification at a subsequent date. In certain situations, a State that was not a participating State, may be allowed to accede to a Convention. In this chapter it is proposed to touch principally on two Conventions which directly affect notaries public namely, The Hague Convention Abolishing the Requirement of Legalisation for Foreign Public Documents concluded at The Hague on 5 October 1961 ('the Hague Convention of 5 October 1961') and the Convention Abolishing the Legalisation of Documents in the Member States of the European Communities concluded at Brussels on 25 May 1987 ('the EC Convention of 25 May 1987'). Both Conventions apply to public documents only. Neither Convention was in force in Ireland at the time of publication of the principal work.

Legalisation: Position in Ireland prior to 1999

The traditional rule of *acte probant sese ipsa* in relation to accepting the authenticity of formal documents was observed in Ireland but was largely confined to documents originating in Ireland or the United Kingdom and intended for use in domestic transactions. It was unlikely, however, that contracting parties, regulatory authorities, government departments and the courts of any state would be prepared, without further ado, to apply the rule of *acte probant sese ipsa* in relation to foreign documents i.e. documents received in the state which had been executed outside the state. All states, therefore, insisted that the highest degree of proof of authenticity should be forthcoming from the state from which a document emanated before it would be acted upon in the receiving state. It was in meeting this standard of proof that the process described under international law as 'legalisation' came into being. Consequently, commencing with verification of the first signature to the document and ending with the last – invariably that of the diplomatic or consular representative of the state in which the document was to be received and acted upon – an unbroken chain of verifications had to be established. The term 'legalisation', however, proved to be an imprecise term to describe the probative procedures used to establish the authenticity of signatures on formal documents and the capacity in which they were made. With the passage of time, individual stages in the verification process came to be referred to as legalisation rather than the completed process. Indeed, the term legalisation came to have different meanings in different countries. In Ireland, when a formal document executed here was required to be produced in a foreign country, the steps necessary to effect legalisation were as follows: the document was executed by or on behalf of the maker or contracting party in Ireland; such execution was then attested by an independent witness or a notary public; in the case of an independent witness, his, or her, signature was attested by a notary public; in either case, the notary's status, signature and (if applied) seal, were certified by the Registrar of the Supreme Court under the seal of the Chief Justice; the signature of the Registrar of the Supreme Court and the seal affixed to the document were verified for the purpose of legalisation by an authorised officer of the Department of Foreign Affairs whose signature and seal were verified for the purposes of legalisation by a diplomatic or consular representative of the state in which the document was intended to be produced. The chain of verifications, as described, having been completed, legalisation could then be said to have been duly effected.

Over time, the delays and inconvenience associated with legalisation began to affect international relations and towards the end of the 1950s the Hague Conference on Private International Law, at the request of the Council of Europe, undertook an examination of legalisation process and the disadvantages associated with its operation. It was from this examination that the Hague Convention on the Abolition of Legalisation for Foreign Public Documents of 5 October 1961 emerged and the Apostille certificate came into existence. The Convention did not abolish legalisation in general. It simply removed that element of the legalisation process which previously had required the diplomatic or consular agent of the state in which a public document[3] was to be produced to authenticate the signature subscribed to the public document and the capacity in which the person signing the document had acted. Article 3 of the Convention stipulates that in order to verify the authenticity of a signature to a public document (and, where appropriate, the seal it bears) the only formality required is the addition of the Apostille of the competent authority of the state from which the document emanates. Ireland did not sign the Hague Convention until 1999. As explained later in this chapter, the EC Convention of 25 May 1987 made further ameliorating inroads into the process of legalisation as regards Ireland and a number of other EC member states.

The Hague Convention of 5 October 1961: Introduction of the Apostille

The Hague Convention of 5 October 1961 ('the Convention'), though open for signature by Ireland since 1961, was signed on behalf of Ireland on 29 October 1996 and ratified on 8 January 1999. It entered into force in the State on 9 March 1999. Under the Convention each contracting state exempts from 'legalisation' public documents emanating from another contracting state which have to be produced in its territory. In this context legalisation means only the formality by which the diplomatic or consular agents of the country in which the document has to be produced certify the authenticity of the signature, the capacity in which the signatory has acted and, where appropriate, the identity of the seal or stamp which it bears. (Article 2). In simple terms, what the Convention abolishes is the intervention of diplomatic or consular representatives of the receiving state as part of the authentication process of public documents.

---

[3] See definition in Chapter 2 *ante*

Prior to Ireland ratifying the Convention, the signature and seal of its consular officer applied to a public document leaving the State would usually have had to be authenticated (legalised) by the diplomatic or consular representative of the state in which the document was to be produced. Legalisation in general was not abolished under the Convention. It continues to be required by states that are not contracting states to the Convention (or the EC Convention of 25 May 1987) and, even as between contracting states, in respect of foreign private documents unless the private documents are notarised, whereupon the notarial act becomes a public document. The Convention, having abolished the requirement of legalisation for foreign public documents, introduced a compensating procedure for the greater comfort of all contracting states. This new procedure is the Apostille (certificate) which must be applied to the public document by the competent authority of the state from which the document emanates. Article 3 of the Convention states, as regards the authentication of a public document, the only formality that may be required in order to certify the authenticity of the signature, the capacity in which the person signing the document has acted and, where appropriate, the identity of the seal or stamp which it bears, is the addition of the certificate described in Article 4 i.e. the Apostille, issued by the competent authority of the State from which the document emanates. The Department of Foreign Affairs was duly designated the competent authority of Ireland for the purpose of administering the Apostille procedure and issuing Apostille certificates on behalf of the State. Consequently, in situations to which the Convention applies, a notarial act of an Irish notary public, being a 'public document', will be verified by having the Apostille stamp applied to the document on which the notarial act is done. The Apostille will confirm that the public document has been signed by the named notary acting in the capacity of a notary public and may identify the notary's seal or stamp. No prior verification of the notary's status, signature or seal by the Supreme Court Office is required[4]; and no verification of the appointment of the

---

[4] The signature and seal of a notary public are verified by a certificate signed by the Registrar of the Supreme Court issued under the seal of the Chief Justice.

Department of Foreign Affairs as the competent authority or of its authorised signatories i.e. consular officers, may be sought other than in exceptional circumstances. A model of an Apostille is reproduced at the end of this chapter. The Apostille must contain the word 'Apostille' in its title and, in French, the words 'Convention de La Haye du octobre 1961' followed by ten standard items of information namely:

1. The name of the country issuing the Apostille in relation to the public document.
2. The name of the person who has signed the public document e.g. the notary public.
3. The capacity in which the person has signed the public document.
4. The fact that the document bears the seal or stamp of the person who executed it.
5. Following the word 'Certified', the place at which the Apostille is issued.
6. The date on which the Apostille is issued.
7. The name of the competent authority e.g. Department of Foreign Affairs.
8. The official number given to the Apostille in the register.
9. The seal or stamp of the competent authority.
10. The signature of the consular officer authorised to sign the Apostille.

From time to time, notaries query why the Apostille issued by the Department of Foreign Affairs leaves item 4 blank notwithstanding that the notary has signed and sealed the public document in question. The Permanent Bureau of the Hague Conference on Private International Law has attempted to explain this practice by stating that for an Apostille to be valid, item 4 of the form of certificate does not have to be completed. This item must only be completed when and if the Apostille certifies the identity of the seal or stamp on the underlying public document. Where the Apostille certifies the authenticity of the signature and, or, capacity in which the person signing the public document has acted, items 2 or 3 apply and it is not necessary to complete item 4. The Bureau further explains that the facility to opt out of completing item 4 has its basis in the use of the words 'where appropriate' in Articles 2 and 3 of the Convention. In other words, the primary focus is on the authentication of signatures and the capacity in which they are made. The use of official seals by notaries and other authorised persons in verifying documents is not standard practice in non-common law countries. The explanation is far from persuasive.

A list of the countries that have signed, acceded to or ratified the Hague Convention of 5 October 1961 or which otherwise recognise the Convention is set forth at the end of this chapter. As additional countries accede to or ratify the Convention, changes may from time to time be made to the list. Accordingly, a notary who is in any doubt as regards the status of a country in relation to the Hague Convention should seek clarification from the Consular Section of the Department of Foreign Affairs at Hainault House, 69-71 St. Stephen's Green, Dublin 2.

Legalisation: Position post 1999

The Hague Convention of 5 October 1961, which came into force in Ireland on 9 March 1999, did not abolish legalisation as an internationally accepted means of establishing the authenticity of foreign documents i.e. documents executed in one state which are intended to be produced in another state. The Convention applies to public documents (as defined in Article 1) only and exempts such documents from one aspect of the traditional legalisation process, namely the diplomatic or consular formality, and introduces the Apostille certificate of the competent authority of the state from which the document emanates as an assurance of the authenticity of the signature to the document. The solemn act of a notary public in attesting a signature to an instrument constitutes a public document within the meaning of the Convention and, on that basis, will be authenticated by an Apostille certificate. As previously explained in this chapter the term 'legalisation' (outside the confines of the Hague Convention) is capable of different meanings. It is sometimes used to describe the completed stages or links in the chain of verifications used to establish the authenticity of a document; while on other occasions it is used to describe any procedural link in that chain. The meaning or usage of the term may also vary from state to state. It is for that reason that legalisation is said to be an imprecise term frequently requiring clarification from those who seek it. Legalisation, therefore, continues to be the appropriate process for establishing the authenticity of private documents which have not been notarised, documents which do not come within the definition of public documents in Article 1 of the Hague Convention of 5 October 1961 and documents, whether public or not, executed in a state that has not signed, acceded to or ratified the Hague Convention, and documents, wherever executed, which are intended to be produced in a state that does not recognise the Convention. In Ireland, when a requirement for legalisation arises, the procedure as outlined above in respect of the pre-1999 position is followed. The notary attests the signature or other form of execution of the document by the maker or contracting party; the notary's status, signature and, if sealed, the seal, are then certified by the Registrar of the Supreme Court under the seal of the Chief Justice. The document is then seen at the Department of Foreign Affairs and the signature of the Registrar of the Supreme Court is certified for the purposes of legalisation by a consular officer at the Department. The signature of the consular officer and seal of the Department of Foreign Affairs is then verified by the diplomatic or consular agent or representative of the state in which the document is to be produced and acted upon.

Under the European Convention on the Abolition of Legalisation of Documents Executed by Diplomatic Agents or Consular Officers, 1968 (which came into force in Ireland on 9 March 1999) legalisation of such documents is abolished as between contracting states of the Council of Europe. Accordingly, a document bearing the signature of an Irish diplomatic or consular officer would be exempt from further legalisation in the state in which it is to be produced if such state has signed or ratified this Convention.

The EC Convention of 25 May 1987 (the 'Convention')

This Convention, which has as its objective the free movement of public documents between member states of the European Communities was ratified by Ireland on 8 December 1998 and came into force in Ireland with effect from 9 March 1999. The Convention exempts from any form of legalisation 'or further formality', public documents executed in one contracting state intended to be produced in another contracting state. 'Public documents' has the same meaning as in the Hague Convention of 5 October 1961 and 'legalisation' has a corresponding meaning to that given to that term in the same Convention. Consequently, in the case of a notarial act (which is a public document), there is no requirement for any further verification or certification of the notary's signature or seal of office. This exemption extends to the Apostille. However, under Article 4 of the Convention, as an exceptional matter, the authorities of the contracting state in which a notarised document is produced may seek information direct from the central authority of the contracting State in which the document has been executed and notarised in respect of the authenticity of the signature (or seal) of the notary public to such document. As between Ireland and Belgium, Denmark, France and Italy the requirement of legalisation, in any form, or the Apostille, to verify notarial signatures and seals on public documents has been completely abolished. The Department of Foreign Affairs (Consular Section) has been designated the Central Authority of the State for the purposes of the Convention.

Consequential amendments to the Rules of the Superior Courts following ratification of Conventions

As a consequence of Ireland's ratification of three international conventions namely, the Convention Abolishing the Legalisation of Documents in the Member States of the European Communities (reviewed above under 'EC Convention of 25 May 1987'), the European Convention on the Abolition of Legalisation of Documents Executed by Diplomatic Agents or Consular Officers of 7 June, 1968 and the Convention Abolishing the Requirement of Legalisation for Foreign Public Documents (reviewed above under 'The Hague Convention of 5 October 1961'), new rules of court entitled 'Rules of the Superior Courts (No.1), (Proof of Foreign Diplomatic, Consular and Public Documents), 1999' were made by Statutory Instrument No. 3 of 1999 and added to the existing rules as Parts VII, VIII and IX of Order 39 of the Rules of the Superior Courts.

Rule 52 of Order 39 of the Rules of the Superior Courts (added as Part VII) directs at paragraph (2) that in the case of a document to which the Convention Abolishing the Legalisation of Documents in the Member States of the European Communities concluded 25 May 1987 applies, the document shall, without further proof of any formal procedure for certifying the authenticity of a signature, the capacity in which the person signing the document has acted, or, where appropriate, the identity of the seal or stamp which it bears, be admissible in evidence as such, provided it is otherwise admissible. Paragraph (3) of the Rule reserves the right of the court in the case of serious doubts (based on good reasons) to question the authenticity of the signature to a document, the capacity in which the signatory has acted or the identity of the seal or stamp it bears. This provision mirrors a similar reservation contained in the Convention. Any such reservation must be directed to the Central Authority of the state from which the document emanated and must disclose the foundation for such reservation. The Rule further directs that, where appropriate, and to the extent required, the provisions of Order 40, Rule 7 of the Rules of the Superior Courts shall apply *mutatis mutandis* to the taking of judicial notice of the seal and signature, as the case may be, of any diplomatic or consular representative or agent, judge, court or notary public lawfully authorised to administer oaths in any of the contracting states.

In the case of a document to which the European Convention on the Abolition of Legalisation of Documents Executed by Diplomatic Agents or Consular Officers concluded on 7 June 1968 applies, Rule 53 of Order 39 of the Rules of the Superior Courts (added as Part VIII) provides at paragraph (2) that such a document, if purporting to have been executed by the diplomatic agents or consular officers of a contracting state, shall without further proof of any formality used to certify the authenticity of the signature on such a document, the capacity in which the person signing such a document has acted, and where appropriate, the identity of the seal or stamp which such document bears, be admissible in evidence without further proof, provided it is otherwise admissible.

Rule 54 of Order 39 of the Rules of the Superior Courts (added as Part IX) provides at paragraph (2) that a document which purports to be an Apostille duly issued and executed in a Contracting State in accordance with the Convention Abolishing the Requirement of Legalisation for Foreign Public Documents concluded on 5 October 1961 shall, without further proof, be deemed to be an Apostille so issued and shall be admissible as evidence of the facts stated therein unless the contrary is shown.

Companies Acts

In Chapter 8 of the principal work reference is made at pages 110-111 to the manner in which constitutional and other official documents of a company e.g. memorandum and articles of association, resolutions etc., may be authenticated by a director, secretary or other authorised officer of the company under the provisions of section 42 of the Companies Act, 1963. It is further pointed out that where such documents are required for production outside the State, it is likely that any such authenticating signature will have to be notarised, followed by legalisation or the application of the Apostille, as appropriate. The Companies Registration Office ('CRO') may issue, for production in foreign countries, officially certified copies of documents that are filed in the CRO. In this case, the signature of the Registrar of Companies (or other authorised CRO official who certifies the documents) will be verified by the Department of Foreign Affairs either by way of legalisation or the application of the Apostille depending on the status of the country in which the documents are to be produced under the Hague Convention of 5 October 1961 or the EC Convention of 25 May 1987.

External or Overseas Companies

Part XI of the Companies Act, 1963 (No. 33 of 1963) applies to companies incorporated outside the State which establish a place of business within the State, sometimes described as external or overseas companies. The certification of constitutional documents filed by such companies in the CRO is governed by section 352 of the Companies Act, 1963 and the relevant statutory procedures are contained in the Companies (Forms) (Amendment) Order, 1999 (S.I. No. 14 of 1999) which amended the Companies (Forms) Order, 1964 (S.I. No. 45 of 1964) with effect from 9 March 1999 to coincide with the ratification by Ireland of the three Conventions referred to in this chapter.

Companies (Forms) (Amendment) Order, 1999

In order to reflect the changes in the way in which foreign public documents are authenticated following on Ireland's ratification of three international conventions, namely the EC Convention of 25 May 1987, the European Convention on the Abolition of Legalisation of Documents executed by Diplomatic or Consular Officers, of 7 June 1968 and the Hague Convention of 5 October 1961, new Articles, numbered 4 to 4E respectively, were substituted by the above Order for the provisions previously contained in Article 4 of the Companies (Forms) Order, 1964. The new Articles provide that a copy of the charter, statutes, memorandum and articles of association of a company, or other instrument constituting or defining the constitution of a company, shall, for the purposes of section 352 of the Companies Act, 1963, be certified a true copy in the state in which the company is incorporated (the 'relevant state') in one of the following ways namely:

1. By an official of the government of the relevant state to whose custody the original of such document is committed, or
2. By a notary of the relevant state, or
3. On oath by some officer of the company before a person having authority to administer an oath.

Except as provided hereunder, the signature, stamp or seal of the official, notary or other person giving the certificate or, as the case may be, administering the oath, and the capacity in which he or she acts, shall be authenticated by an Irish diplomatic or consular officer. This requirement shall not apply where the relevant state is a state in which the EC Convention of 25 May 1987 is in force or, if not so in force, is a state in which the European Convention on the Abolition of Legalisation of Documents Executed by Diplomatic Agents or Consular Officers is in force and the official, notary or other person giving the certificate or administering the oath is a diplomatic or consular officer of the relevant state acting in his or her official capacity; or, the relevant state is a state in which the Hague Convention of 5 October 1961 is in force, in which case the Apostille certificate issued under Article 4 of the Convention shall be used in lieu of the form of authentication referred to above.

Companies giving Powers of Attorney

At page 108 of the principal work, it is stated that under section 40 of the Companies Act, 1963 (Section 34 of the Companies Act, (Northern Ireland) 1960) provision is made for a company to appoint an attorney for the purpose of executing deeds abroad on the company's behalf. Due to Ireland's extensive and expanding business interests outside the State, the execution of such powers of attorney is now a frequent occurrence. The power of attorney will usually require to be notarised and, depending on the country in which it is to be produced, to have the notary's signature legalised or an Apostille certificate applied. If the notary public is present when the company seals the power of attorney, he or she may make out a notarial certificate as an attesting witness. However, the beneficiary of the power of attorney, or the regulatory authorities of the country in which it is to be produced, may require other matters concerning the company, not within the knowledge of the notary, to be averred to. For this reason, it is considered more appropriate that the secretary or a director or other officer of the company should complete any such averment and that the notary confine himself or herself to attesting the signature of such person. A short form of notarial certificate is contained in Appendix 7 to this supplement. Other forms are contained in appendices 45, 46 and 47 - Section D of the principal work. The European Communities (Companies) Regulations, 1973 (S.I. No. 163 of 1973) make provision for the registration in the CRO of the name and description of a person who has been authorised by a company to effect binding obligations on the company's behalf. A power of attorney given by an Irish company in favour of a person empowered to execute a deed on the company's behalf would come within this regulation and company solicitors should note accordingly.

Model Apostille Certificate

APOSTILLE
(Convention de La Haye du 5 octobre 1961)

1. Country: ....
This public document
2. has been signed by ....
3. acting in the capacity of ....
4. bears the seal/stamp of ....
....

Certified

5. at ....   6. the ....
7. by ....
8. No. ....
9. Seal/Stamp: 10. Signature:

Countries, Territories and Departments in which the Hague Convention of 5 October 1961 is in operation or otherwise recognised

(In alphabetical order)

A. Albania, American Samoa, Andorra, Angola, Anguilla, Antigua and Barbuda, Argentina, Armenia, Aruba, Australia, Austria, Azerbaijan, Azores

B. Bahamas, Barbados, Belarus, Belgium, Belize, Bermuda, Bosnia and Herzegovina, Botswana, British Antartic Territory, British Virgin Islands, Brunei Darussalam, Bulgaria

C. Cayman Islands, Colombia, Croatia, Cyprus, Czech Republic

D. Djibouti, Dominica

E. Ecuador, El Salvador, Estonia

F. Falkland Islands, Fiji, Finland, France, French Polynesia (Fr. Territory)

G. Germany, Gibraltar (UK Territory), Greece, Grenada, Guadeloupe (Fr. Department), Guam, Guernsey, Guiana (French Guyana), Guyana.

H. Honduras, Hong Kong (SAR), Hungary

I. Iceland, India, Ireland, Isle of Man (UK Territory), Israel, Italy

J. Japan, Jersey (UK Territory)

K. Kazakhstan, Kiribati (Gilbert Islands)

L. Latvia, Lesotho, Liberia, Liechtenstein, Lithuania, Luxembourg

M. Macau (SAR), Macedonia, Madeira, Malawi, Malta, Marshall Islands, Martinique (Fr. Department), Mauritius, Mayotte (Fr. Department), Mexico, Monaco, Montserrat, (UK Territory), Mozambique

N. Namibia, Netherlands, Netherlands Antilles (Dtch. Territory), New Caledonia (Fr. Territory), New Zealand, Niue, Northern Mariana Islands (US Territory), Norway

P. Panama, Poland, Portugal, Puerto Rico (US Territory)

R. Reunion (Fr. Department), Romania, Russian Federation

S. Samoa, San Marino, St. Helena (UK Territory), St. Kitts and Nevis, St. Lucia, St. Pierre and Miquelon (Fr. Territory), St. Vincent and The Grenadines, Serbia and Montenegro, Seychelles, South Georgia and South Sandwich Islands (UK Territory), Slovakia, Slovenia, Solomon Islands, South Africa, Spain (including the Canary Islands), Suriname, Swaziland, Sweden, Switzerland

T. Tonga, Trinidad and Tobago, Turkey, Turks and Caicos Islands (UK Territory), Tuvalu

U. Ukraine, United Kingdom, United States of America, United States Virgin Islands (US Territory)

V. Vanuatu, Venezuela

W. Wallis and Futuna (Fr. Territory)

Z. Zimbabwe

Note: In some of the countries and territories listed above, legalisation of the Apostille certificate by their Consulate may be still be required.

Chapter 12

FOREIGN ADOPTION
Role of the Notary Public

This chapter is not intended to provide a definitive statement of the law governing foreign adoption now more frequently described as inter-country adoption. Its purpose is to explain, for the benefit of the reader, the main features of current Irish legislation in this area and the investigative process that intending adopters must undergo in order to satisfy domestic and foreign adoption authorities as to their eligibility and suitability to be adoptive parents. The chapter concludes with an explanation of the role of the notary in the adoption process.

Foreign Adoption - Pre 1991
The principal work did not deal with foreign adoption. In the first place, prior to the late 1980s, the number of foreign adoptions involving Irish residents was relatively small. Secondly, there was no statutory framework in existence in Ireland under which foreign adoptions could be given full legal recognition. The Adoption Act, 1952, which deals with domestic adoptions, did not extend to foreign adoptions. During the 1980s, due to changes in social attitudes and improvements in the welfare system, the numbers of Irish born children being offered for adoption dwindled to such an extent that the needs of Irish couples, seeking to adopt, could no longer be satisfied from within the State. Consequently, despite the absence of a statutory framework, more and more Irish couples began to look abroad for children whom they might adopt. Then, in 1989, Romania opened its doors to foreign adopters and in a short period of time more 'adopted' children were being brought into the State from Romania on a weekly basis than might previously have been brought here in an entire year.

When the surge of Romanian adoptions commenced in the late 1980s, no official procedures were in place in Ireland for assessing the eligibility and suitability of persons intending to adopt abroad.

Consequently, with little or no preparation, in the form of advice, guidance or counselling, Irish adopters set out on their journey into unchartered territory with a mixture of hope and apprehension. On arrival, operating through local adoption agencies, they sought out a child available for adoption. Having found a child, they negotiated the terms of the child's adoption with the local adoption agency following which they appeared before a local court for the purpose of securing approval of the adoption and leave to remove the child from Romania. Then they travelled back to Ireland with their 'adopted' child. These adoptions, though apparently valid under Romanian law, were not recognised under Irish law.

Adoption Act, 1991 - Introduction of New Procedures
The legal anomalies arising from non-recognition of foreign adoptions demanded urgent remedial action. Relief came in 1991 when the whole area of foreign adoptions was given a proper legal framework by the Adoption Act, 1991 (No. 14 of 1991). This Act enabled existing irregular foreign adoptions to be regularised under Irish law and provided the necessary statutory framework for all future foreign adoptions involving couples of Irish domicile or residence. The Act authorised the making of Adoption Orders (as defined in the Adoption Act, 1952) in respect of foreign adoptions, including adoptions made before the commencement of the Act, provided such adoptions were deemed lawful under the law of the place in which the adoption was effected and otherwise met certain criteria laid down in the Act.

The Act made provision for the Adoption Board to establish and maintain a Register of Foreign Adoptions in which particulars of foreign adoptions by persons domiciled or resident in the State were henceforth to be entered. Registration rights were also extended to Irish couples either of whom was domiciled or habitually resident in the country where the adoption was effected. The drive for the introduction and enactment of the new legislation was spearheaded by the then Deputy Alan Shatter, T.D., a solicitor with a deep understanding of adoption problems, who had worked tirelessly in promoting the Bill.

Eligibility and Suitability Tests
Under the new regime introduced under the Adoption Act, 1991 (as amended by the Adoption Act, 1998), persons intending to adopt a child must be able to prove that they fall within one of the categories of persons eligible to be adopters and then undergo a rigorous assessment (the Home Study Programme) to determine their suitability to be adopters. Such assessments are carried out by the appropriate Health Service Executive Area (formerly by the appropriate Health Boards) or by a registered Adoption Society. Eligibility is determined generally by reference to marital status, consanguinity or other relationship based on, or arising from, marriage. Intending adopters must be over 21 years of age and be ordinarily resident in the State. Suitability is based on the intending adopter(s) being able to satisfy, by means of their assessment, the criteria contained in section 13 of the Adoption Act, 1952. The new system brought clarity, order and professional expertise to bear on the adoption system in Ireland. This has operated for the benefit of all concerned including the governments of countries which have opened their doors to foreign or intercountry adoptions.

One positive effect of the procedures introduced under the Adoption Act, 1991 (as amended and extended by the Adoption Act, 1998) is that persons going abroad to adopt a child are much better prepared for what lies ahead; and the risk of having a disappointing or traumatic experience is substantially reduced.

Document Dossier
Persons who have obtained from the Adoption Board a declaration of eligibility and suitability, (based on the report of their assessment by the appropriate Health Services Executive or a registered Adoption Society - the Home Study Programme) and who are in possession of an Immigration Certificate, may commence the next stage of preparations namely, to satisfy the regulations and procedures of the authorities of the foreign country or place in which the adoption is to be effected. This can be an onerous and time consuming task as the official requirements may vary from place to place - even within the same country. One might be forgiven for believing that the declaration as to eligibility and suitability issued

by the Adoption Board, together with an Immigration Certificate and Letter of Introduction, would be all that might be necessary before intending adopters set off for the foreign country in which the adoption is to be effected. This, however, is not the case and on deeper consideration it is understandable, and indeed logical, that the authorities of the foreign country should be no less diligent than the Irish authorities in their examination of the primary source material offered in support of the adoption of any of its citizens. Consequently, in addition to the documents mentioned, intending adopters are obliged to assemble a dossier containing verified or verifiable information as regards many other matters e.g. their birth, marriage, health, character, residence and domestic accommodation, occupation, financial state, asset worth, transport facilities etc., A letter of undertaking from the Health Service Executive promising continuing post-adoption supervision of the adopted child is frequently requested. The list appears to be open-ended at the discretion of the country or place in which an adoption is to be effected and this is likely to remain the position in the absence of a convention or a bilateral intercountry agreement which specifies the documents to be provided in support of an adoption application.

Based on the information requirements identified in the previous paragraph, it is likely that the prospective adopters' document dossier will comprise of most, if not all, of the following documents:

1. Adoption Board certificate of eligibility and suitability;
2. Health Service Executive (or a registered Adoption Society) Home Study Adoption Social Report;
3. Immigration clearance letter issued by the Department of Justice, Equality and Law Reform;
4. Marriage certificate (civil) of adopters;[5]
5. Birth certificate of male adopter - long form - issued by the Registrar of Births etc.;
6. Birth certificate of female adopter - long form -issued by the Registrar of Births etc.;

---

[5] For the sake of convenience the term 'adopter' is used for 'prospective adopter' elsewhere in this chapter.

7. Extract from male adopter's current passport (including number, issuance details and photograph);
8. Extract from female adopter's current passport (including number, issuance details and photograph);
9. Garda Síochána/Police clearance letter (from age 12) *re* male adopter;
10. Garda Síochána/Police clearance letter (from age 12) *re* female adopter;
11. Medical certificate verifying physical and mental state of health of male adopter;
12. Medical certificate verifying physical and mental state of health of female adopter;
13. Medical certificate verifying infertility;
14. Employer's certificate as to employment and income of male adopter;
15. Employer's certificate as to employment and income of female adopter (if applicable).

In addition to the documents enumerated above, the following will usually be required:

1. Undertaking from the appropriate Health Service Executive area to continue the supervision of the adopted child for a number of years after arrival in Ireland;
2. Letter of introduction from the Adoption Board to the foreign authority or adoption agency;
3. Statement and valuation of adopters' assets;
4. Verification (some countries) of the identity, signature and official status i.e. chairmanship, of the chairman of the Adoption Board.

Anticipated Legislative Change

The Hague Convention on Protection of Children and Co-Operation in Respect of Intercountry Adoption (concluded 29 May 1993), which Ireland has signed, may eventually provide a standard list of documentary proofs as between participating States. The list may not be much shorter than under the present arrangements but, at least, it should be conclusive. The information concerning the adopters specified in Article 15 of the Convention includes 'identity, eligibility and suitability to adopt, background, family and medical history, social environment, reasons for adoption, ability to undertake an intercountry adoption, as well as the characteristics of the children for whom they would be qualified to care', all of which must form part of the report submitted to the Central Authority of the receiving State e.g. Ireland, to be transmitted to the Central Authorities of the State of origin i.e. the place in which the adoption is to be effected. It is intended that the Convention will be enacted into Irish law and heads of a Bill have been approved by the Government at the time of writing.

The Role of the Notary in the Foreign Adoption Process

The notary's involvement in the foreign adoption process will usually commence with a telephone call enquiring if the notary is available to notarise a 'set of adoption papers'. The notary should make an estimate of the amount of time that should be made available in relation to notarising the documents; such estimate should include the time it may take to get responses from the authors of any of the papers or documents about which the notary may have reasonable concern. If, as frequently is the case, the adoption papers have to be held overnight, the notary should assure the adopters of the safety of their papers and explain how the need to hold them overnight arises. In the telephone conversation setting up the appointment, the intending adopters should be requested to bring with them their current passports and a utility bill (to establish identity and place of residence) together with the originals (for comparison purposes) of any documents they intend to retain, while using certified copies in lieu. While the notary has a duty to check the nature and completeness of each document produced before him in support of the adopters' application, this should not be done in such a way as to create the impression that the notary is prying into the adopters' private lives, medical histories or financial affairs. In general, the notary will rely on visual examination in determining the genuineness of the documents presented in support of the adoption application. The notary, however, may extend such examination by seeking further information or confirmation should circumstances deem it appropriate.

The notary, having examined the adopters' document dossier, will determine which of the documents purport to be originals and which are copies of documents that purport to be originals. In the case of the latter, the notary will require sight of the original document so that the copy may be compared with it. The current practice of some notaries is to 'note' each document, whether original or copy, by subscribing his or her name across a Faculty adhesive wafer seal affixed to the document signing partly over the seal and partly on the paper itself, inserting the corresponding document number as in the schedule, followed by the date and the notary's stamp or, if appropriate, the notary's seal. When all the documents have been assembled and bound in booklet form, the notary will authenticate them by means of a notarial certificate issued under his or her official seal to be attached to the front of the booklet. The certificate should be substantially in the form of the precedent in Appendix 9 to this supplement. Depending on the status under the Hague Convention of 5 October 1961 of the country in which the adopters are seeking a child for adoption, the completed document dossier, together with the notarial certificate, will have to be processed through the Department of Foreign Affairs in Ireland for legalisation or to have the Apostille certificate applied. The Department has capped consular fees in adoption matters at 50 euro irrespective of the number of documents that require to be legalised or apostilled.

Country by Country (2006)

Russia currently accounts for the largest number of all inter-country adoptions. Between 2001-2005 over 600 children were adopted from Russia and the Adoption Board is currently pursuing a bi-lateral agreement with the Russian Federation. Romania closed its doors to Irish adopters in 2001 and Belarus is at the time of writing also closed. Ukraine is open, but has its own rules governing adoptions. India is open but has no bilateral agreement with Ireland and no adoption orders, as such, are made by India. Bilateral agreements or other forms of working arrangements are in place between Ireland and China, Thailand, Philippines and Vietnam. Under the bilateral agreement between Ireland and Vietnam a fee, currently €6,000, must be paid by the adopters through the Irish Mediation Agency to the local provisional governments in Vietnam to be applied for child welfare, support and education. In 2004 there were 461 declarations of eligibility and suitability issued by the Adoption Board. This number fell by 10% in 2005 and indications for 2006 suggest a further fall. Any decline in numbers is more likely to be attributable to administrative delays in the processing of applications rather than to a lessening of interest in adoption on the part of Irish couples. There are currently over 1,800 Irish couples waiting to begin the assessment process.

Notarial Fees on Adoptions

In Chapter 5 *ante*, the legal position in regard to fees for notarial services was explained. Because of competition law, there are no scales of fees, set fees or recommended fees for notarial services. This position applies equally when the notary is dealing with an adoption matter. Until the notary can see what is involved in any given case, he or she is not in a position to estimate the amount of professional time that will have to be set aside for the task. No two cases are ever the same. The general principle is that the fee should reasonably reflect the value of the notary's time, skill and responsibility for the work to be undertaken on the same basis as would apply in the case of any other professional service provider.

Chapter 13

MONEY-LAUNDERING

The term 'money-laundering' means the process whereby the identity of money representing the proceeds of criminal conduct is changed ('washed') through apparently legitimate transactions and processes, so that the money appears to originate from a legitimate source. In recent years, concerted efforts have been made on a worldwide basis to restrict the circumstances in which illegal proceeds of crime can be laundered through legitimate business. This has, primarily, taken the form of legislation creating specific new criminal offences and placing obligations on service providers to verify the identity of customers or clients, to maintain records and report suspicious transactions.

Under the provisions of the Criminal Justice Act, 1994 (No. 15 of 1994), as amended, all financial institutions in the State are subject to the provisions of the 1994 Act in terms of its requirements to:

1. Identify clients;
2. Maintain records; and
3. Report suspicious transactions to an Garda Síochána and the Revenue Commissioners.

The most common method used to 'launder' crime proceeds or illegally obtained funds is through the financial system by using cheques and electronic funds transfers. The trend in Ireland has been for individuals to buy expensive property and high value goods, e.g. houses, apartments, commercial buildings, shops, boats and cars. In many cases false documentation will be used, including false identification. Raising substantial monies on mortgages obtained on the basis of false information provided by corrupt professionals is yet-another approach. The mortgage is then redeemed after a period of time using 'dirty' money which then gets into the system.

EU Directive 91/308/EEC brought notaries and other independent legal professionals within the scope of the community anti-money-laundering regime. The Criminal Justice Act, 1994 (Section 32)

Regulations of 2003 (S.I. No. 242 of 2003) designated any person in the State who practises as a solicitor and imposed upon the solicitors' profession, as and from 15 September 2003, the obligation to:

1. Take measures to identify new clients and maintain records of their identity;
2. Maintain records of all relevant transactions by both new and existing clients and keep copies of all documents for at least five years following the completion of the transaction;
3. Introduce internal procedures for staff training and awareness;
4. Introduce internal reporting procedures; and
5. Report suspicious transactions to An Garda Síochána and the Revenue Commissioners.

While notaries have been specifically mentioned in Directive 91/308/EEC and subsequently in the second Directive 2001/97/EEC and the third Directive 2005/60/EEC, the function of the Irish notary was not deemed to be affected by these Directives, or indeed the legislation referred to above, by virtue of the fact that, in general, the Irish notary *qua* notary did not provide legal advice or handle client funds. The main functions of an Irish notary relate principally but not exclusively to:

1. Authenticating public and private documents;
2. Attesting and verifying signatures to documents in order to satisfy evidential or statutory requirements of foreign governments or of overseas institutions and regulatory authorities;
3. Noting and protesting bills of exchange or promissory notes for non acceptance or non payment;
4. Drawing up ships protests;
5. Giving certificates as to the acts and instruments of persons and their identities.

By virtue of the fact that the vast majority of Irish notaries are also solicitors, it is strongly recommended that the Irish notary would follow the obligations that the notary has as a solicitor and that any non-solicitor notaries should also comply with such obligations.

Identity of Appearer

The notary should establish the identity of an appearer who seeks the services of the notary by ensuring that at least two of the following three forms of identity are made available:

1. Passport
2. Driving Licence
3. Utility Bill

All these documents should be in the name of the appearer. On occasions, a letter of introduction from a solicitor may be desirable. On account of the number of forged driving licences that are in existence, it is recommended that a driving licence alone should not be accepted as satisfactory evidence of the identity of the appearer. In the event that the notary is not entirely satisfied with the authenticity of the documents produced to prove the identity of the appearer, the notary should request a letter of introduction from a solicitor or else decline to perform the notarial act.

It is recommended that the staff in the notary's office, when making an appointment for a notarial act to be performed, should request the intended appearer to bring with him or her any two of the three identity documents mentioned above.

It may arise from time to time that an appearer is unable to produce either a passport or a driving licence and in the event that the notary is satisfied that there are good reasons for the situation, another form of photo identification should be requested, such as a Garda National Immigration Bureau identity certificate or any of the documents described in Chapter 7 of this supplement in relation to statutory declarations.

When the appearer attends before the notary, a photocopy of the data page of his or her passport, or driving licence, containing a photograph of the appearer should be taken and the appearer should be asked to sign this copy page. The notary should be satisfied as to the physical likeness of the appearer to the photographic identification produced and that the details on the data page appear to be consistent with the appearer.

Maintain Records

The notary should take a photocopy of the appearer's passport or other form of identification or identifying document produced by the appearer together with a photocopy of the document that is the subject of the notarial act. These documents should be kept for a period of not less than five years from the date of the notarial act.

Obligation to Report a Suspicious Transaction

It is recommended that the notary should follow the obligations of a solicitor practising in the State to report a suspicious transaction to An Garda Síochána and the Revenue Commissioners. There is no definition of the words 'suspects' or 'suspicion' in the legislation, nor is there any widely accepted definition as to what the term 'suspicious' means. Ashe and Reid *Money-Laundering Risks and Liabilities*, (Round Hall 2000) offers the following advice:

> 'Once suspicion has been aroused, then the institutions must make a report. There is no scope for thinking "I am not suspicious yet but I am concerned". There is no middle ground. It is all or nothing. Suspicious must also include the concept of "wilful blindness".'

Suspicion does not have to have a basis in admissible evidence. It can legitimately take into account matters which should be excluded in the trial of a case in Court. It is not possible to devise a simple formula that encompasses the obligations of disclosure. The very concept of suspicion defies conclusive definition. A suspicion does not have to relate to every ingredient of the offence. Once a suspicion is raised, a report should be made. Where in doubt, the notary should err on the side of caution and report.

Criminal Justice Act 1994 – Designated Country

There is an inter-governmental body (established at a G-7 Summit in 1989) called Financial Action Task Force (FATF). Initially, it comprised the G-7 countries, the EU Commission and eight other countries. It was established to develop international measures against money-laundering. FATF monitors the progress of member countries in the fight against money-laundering and, more recently, terrorist financing.

FATF published 40 recommendations designed to combat money-laundering, covering the criminal justice system and law enforcement, the financial system and its regulations, and international cooperation. These recommendations have been endorsed by the members of FATF and, while they do not constitute a binding international convention, many countries in the world, including the EU Member States, have made a political commitment to implement them. It is from these 40 recommendations that the EU Directives on money-laundering implemented in Ireland flow.

FATF operates a list of Non-Cooperative Countries and Territories (NCCT), which constantly changes. The list operates as a 'Name and Shame' device to encourage those countries that are not doing enough in the fight against money-laundering to 'clean up their act' and have their name removed from the list. The Criminal Justice (Theft and Fraud Offences) Act, 2001 (No. 50 of 2001) permitted the Irish Government to require automatic reporting of transactions within specified countries and territories. These countries and territories can be readily ascertained by accessing the website www.fatf-gafi.org and click on 'NCCT'. This will give a list of non-cooperative countries and territories. The latest list published as at 23 June 2006 listed Myanmar (formerly Burma) alone.

If the notary is requested to perform a notarial act where the final destination of the notarised document is a country that appears on the NCCT list for the time being, then the notary must automatically report the matter to An Garda Síochána and the Revenue Commissioners.

Law Society Guidelines

The Law Society of Ireland has published excellent guidance notes for solicitors on anti money-laundering legislation. They include an identity and, or, address verification form and a standard reporting form. It is strongly recommended that the notary keeps up-to-date with these guidance notes and any further information circulated by the Law Society of Ireland.

Summary
1. Obtain best photographic identification and keep photocopies.
2. Keep records for a minimum of five years.
3. Report any suspicious transactions.
4. Remember FATF. [See above]

5. Keep up-to-date with Law Society of Ireland Guidelines and any guidelines that may be issued by the Faculty of Notaries Public in Ireland to its members.

Chapter 14

ELECTRONIC COMMERCE

Introduction
Terms such as 'cyberspace' and 'electronic commerce' became commonplace in the 1990s. 'Cyberspace' is the term usually attributed to science-fiction writer, William Gibson, in *Neuromancer* (1984). Cyberspace is regarded as a description (in part) for that nebulous territory without physical dimensions where 'electronic communications' happen, including where communications over the Internet are transmitted, some in real time, some delayed, involving various telecommunications and computing technologies.

During the 1990s, the American Bar Association and its section on Science and Technology Law made submissions to agencies of Government of the United States that there should be a new public officer known as a 'cybernotary' whose role would be one in which technical and legal expertise would be combined and who would serve complementary functions associated with the traditional role of the notary together with a certain level of qualification on information security technology. The cybernotary would be empowered to certify electronically and authenticate elements of an electronic commercial transaction which would facilitate its enforceability under relevant laws.

Cybernotarial Ireland Ltd.
In 1995, influenced by developments in the United States and Europe, the Faculty of Notaries Public in Ireland established a separate company called Cybernotarial Ireland Ltd. The principal object of this company was:

> 'The promotion, advancement and regulation of those members of the professional body of notaries public practising in the Republic of Ireland and Northern Ireland as are desirous of becoming proficient in cybernotarial knowledge and membership of the proposed international cybernotarial organisation…'

In reality, the cybernotary as a distinct profession and the proposed international cybernotarial organisation never materialised. However, during the 1990s and in 2000 there were several major developments in the law governing electronic commerce.

International Developments

On an international level, the European Signatures Directive (Directive on a Community Framework for Electronic Signatures (1999/93/EC) provided a legal framework for electronic signatures and endeavoured to harmonise the legal acceptance of electronic signatures throughout the European Union. This Directive was adopted on 13 December 1999 and came into force on 19 January 2000.

The Electronic Commerce Directive (2000/31/ EC) regulated contracting on-line and other legal aspects of electronic commercial communications. Essentially, the Electronic Commerce Directive endeavoured to facilitate e-business throughout the European Union and to protect consumers in relation to contracting on-line. The Electronic Commerce Directive was adopted on 8 June 2000 and entered into force on 17 July 2000. The Oireachtas enacted the Electronic Commerce Act, 2000 (No. 27 of 2000) and implemented the European Signatures Directive and transposed into domestic law certain articles of the Electronic Commerce Directive, referred to above.

The Electronic Commerce Act, 2000

The Electronic Commerce Act, 2000 ('the 2000 Act') was enacted to provide for the legal recognition of electronic contracts, electronic writing, electronic signatures and original information in electronic form in relation to commercial and non-commercial transactions. The 2000 Act also dealt with the admissibility of evidence in relation to such matters (set out above), as well as the accreditation, supervision and liability of certification service providers and the registration of domain names. The 2000 Act was also based on certain provisions of the United Nations International Communication on Trade Law known as the UNICTRAL Model Law on E-Commerce 1996, revised in 1998.

Definitions in the Electronic Commerce Act, 2000

It may be useful to give some definitions here which are set out in the Electronic Commerce Act, 2000:

'Advanced electronic signature' is defined as meaning an electronic signature:

(a) uniquely linked to the signatory,
(b) capable of identifying the signatory,
(c) created using means that are capable of being maintained by the signatory under his, or her, or its sole control and
(d) linked to the data to which it relates in such a manner that any subsequent change of the data is detectable.

'Certificate' means 'an electronic attestation which links signature verification data to a person or public body, and confirms the identity of the person or public body'.

'Certification service provider' means 'a person or public body who issues certificates or provides other services related to electronic signatures'.

'Electronic' is defined as including 'electrical, digital, magnetic, optical, electromagnetic, biometric, photonic and any other form of related technology'.

'Electronic contract' is defined as 'a contract wholly or partly concluded by means of an electronic communication'.

'Electronic signature' means 'data in any electronic form attached to, incorporated in, or logically associated with other electronic data which serves as a method of authenticating the purported originator and includes an advanced electronic signature'.

'Qualified certificate' means a certificate which fulfils certain technical requirements set out in Annex 1 of the Act and is provided by a certification service provider who fulfils the technical requirements set out in Annex 11 of the Act.

'Signature verification data' means 'data, such as codes, passwords, algorithms or public cryptographic keys, used for the purposes of verifying an electronic signature'.

Fundamental Part of Electronic Commerce Act

Part II of the Electronic Commerce Act, 2000 (section 9) provides that information shall not be denied legal effect, validity or enforceability solely on the grounds that it is wholly or partly in electronic form, whether as an electronic communication or otherwise. In effect, the 2000 Act provides for equivalence between electronic and paper-based systems. This is the fundamental part of the legislation regulating electronic commerce. However, section 10 of the Act of 2000 specifically provides that the electronic commerce enabling provisions of the legislation do not apply (at least initially) to a will, codicil, or other testamentary instrument, a trust, an enduring power of attorney, or a deed in which an interest in real property may be created, acquired, disposed of, or registered, other that contracts for the creation, acquisition or disposal of such interests. Excluded also from the electronic commerce enabling provisions of the 2000 Act is the law governing the making of an affidavit or a statutory or sworn declaration, or the rules, practices or procedures of a court or tribunal. There is specific provision in the Act, however, that where the relevant Minister is of the opinion that technology has advanced to an appropriate extent, and following consultation with other relevant Ministers, the electronic commerce provisions of the 2000 Act may be extended to those excluded categories of legal documents described in this paragraph.

In the context of writing, section 12 of the 2000 Act provides (subject to certain qualifications) that any requirement to provide information in writing, for example, by virtue of the Statute of Frauds (Ireland) 1695, may be met by writing in electronic form. Section 13 of the Act provides that an electronic signature can be used to meet the requirements of a written signature.

In relation to documents required to be under seal, section 16 of the 2000 Act provides that an advanced electronic signature (defined earlier in this chapter) based on a qualified certificate (defined earlier) may be used to meet the requirement that a document be sealed. As to the production or retention of electronic information, section 18 of the 2000 Act provides that electronic information can be used to meet a requirement to produce or retain information that is in the form of paper or other material. In effect, this allows for the retention and subsequent production of documents in electronic format as distinct from the retention or production of such documents in paper format.

Section 19 of the 2000 Act provides, in relation to contracts, that an electronic contract shall not be denied legal effect, validity, or enforceability, solely on the grounds that it is wholly or partly in electronic form, or has been concluded wholly or partly by way of an electronic communication.

Certification Service Providers

Part III of the Electronic Commerce Act, 2000 provides for the accreditation and supervision of certification service providers - a person or public body who issues electronic certificates or who provides other services related to electronic signatures. These service providers supply, *inter alia*, an electronic attestation (certificate) linking signature verification data to a person and also confirm the identity of that person.

The 2000 Act provides (section 20) that a person or public body is not required to obtain the prior authority of any other person or public body to provide certification or other services relating to electronic commerce. Certification service providers are, in effect, free to set up business and offer their services without any licensing regime. The legislation provides that the relevant Minister may introduce voluntary accreditation schemes with a view to improving the level of service offered. However, in relation to certification service providers who issue qualified certificates to the public, section 29 of the 2000 Act provides that the relevant Minister shall prescribe a scheme of supervision of certification service providers established in the State.

eNotarisation and eApostilles

The first International Forum on eNotarisation and eApostilles, jointly organised by the Hague Conference on Private International Law and the International Union of Latin Notaries and hosted by the National Notary Association of the United States took place in Las Vegas, Nevada (United States) in May 2005. Representatives from 31 nations attended. The Forum concluded that an interpretation of the Hague Convention of 5 October 1961, in the light of the principle of functional equivalence, permits competent authorities to keep electronic registers and issue electronic Apostilles to further enhance international legal assistance and government services.

It had been envisaged that the cybernotary, as a trusted third party, would play a significant role in electronically certifying and authenticating all elements of an electronic commercial transaction which would be crucial to the legal enforceability of such a transaction. This may indeed occur at some time. Perhaps, in conclusion, in this context, the writers may paraphrase a wise person who observed that while predictions in relation to technology are often true, the timing of when the predictions will become a reality is often woefully inaccurate.

APPENDICES

APPENDIX 1

(Extract)

RULES OF THE SUPERIOR COURTS (NO.2) OF 1993
S.I. No. 265 of 1993

Addition of Order 127

7. The following shall be inserted as Order 127 of the Rules of the Superior Courts:

ORDER 127

Notaries

1. The Chief Justice may, in exercise of his discretion and from time to time, make such rules and regulations or give such practice directions as he may think fit, as to the form and mode of application to be appointed a notary public.

2. Such rules, regulations or directions may require that an applicant satisfy the Chief Justice in advance of the appointment of the applicant that he had the requisite and appropriate knowledge of notarial practice and procedure.

Citation

8. These rules may be cited as the Rules of the Superior Courts (No.2) of 1993 and shall be construed with the Rules of the Superior Courts.

Commencement

9. These rules shall come into operation on the 9th day of September, 1993.

APPENDIX 1A

DIRECTION

APPOINTMENT OF NOTARIES PUBLIC

In pursuance of the powers vested in me by Order 127 of the Rules of the Superior Courts (No. 2) of 1993, I hereby make the following directions and regulations concerning the application of persons to be appointed a Notary Public.

1. The applicant shall before making application for appointment satisfy the Faculty of Notaries Public in Ireland that he or she has a sufficient knowledge of notarial matters and procedures and of the particular legal provisions applicable to notarial matters to be a competent and efficient person to carry out the duties of a notary public if appointed.
2. In the event of an applicant for appointment as a Notary Public failing to obtain from the Faculty of Notaries Public in Ireland a certificate of competency above referred to the Faculty shall state in writing the reasons why they have declined to grant their certificate.
3. In the event of an intending applicant for appointment as a Notary Public failing to obtain the certificate of competency above referred to he/she shall still be entitled to continue to apply but upon making an application under such circumstances shall exhibit on affidavit the decision issued by the Faculty as to their reasons for declining to grant a certificate and may adduce such other evidence as it is intended to rely upon in making the application with regard to competency.

Thomas A. Finlay
CHIEF JUSTICE

Dated the 28th day of March 1994

APPENDIX 1B

Form 1

THE FACULTY OF NOTARIES PUBLIC IN IRELAND
34 Upper Baggot Street
Dublin 4

CERTIFICATE OF COMPETENCY

(issued by The Faculty of Notaries Public in Ireland for the purposes of Order 127 of the Rules of the Superior Courts (No. 2) of 1993, and in accordance with the Practice Direction of the Chief Justice made on 28th March 1994, to a person intending to apply to be appointed a Notary Public)

Name of Applicant:

Address:

Examination date:

The above named applicant, having been examined by the Examination Body established by The Faculty of Notaries Public in Ireland (the "Faculty") for the purposes of Order 127 of the Rules of the Superior Courts (No. 2) of 1993, has satisfied the Faculty, on the basis of such examination, that (s)he has a sufficient knowledge of notarial matters and procedures and of the particular legal provisions applicable to notarial matters to be a competent and efficient person to carry out the duties of a Notary Public, if appointed.

Dated this   day of   2006

For and on behalf of
The Faculty of Notaries Public
in Ireland

_____
DEAN OF THE FACULTY

APPENDIX 2

PETITION FOR APPOINTMENT AS A NOTARY PUBLIC

TO:
THE CHIEF JUSTICE

IN THE MATTER OF A.B. [SOLICITOR] SEEKING TO BE APPOINTED A NOTARY PUBLIC

AND

IN THE MATTER OF THE COURTS (SUPPLEMENTAL PROVISIONS) ACT, 1961

THE HUMBLE PETITION of A.B. who resides at _____ in the City/County of _____ and practises as a Solicitor at _____ in the City/County of _____ seeking to appointed a Notary Public SHOWETH:

1. Your Petitioner is _____ years of age and was admitted a Solicitor of the Courts in Ireland in the[1] _____ Term of the Year _____, and since admission has been in continuous practice in the following positions[2]:
2. Your Petitioner has obtained a Certificate of Competency from the Faculty of Notaries Public in Ireland in accordance with the Practice Direction of the Chief Justice dated the 28th day of March 1994.
3. Your Petitioner by virtue of the foregoing qualifications and experience has a good understanding of the law and practice in relation to those areas of business and commerce with which a Notary Public is most likely to be concerned.
4. Your Petitioner's practice as a Solicitor brings [him] [her] into regular contact with members of the business community including accountants, bankers, brokers, carriers, forwarding agents, merchants, shipping agents, insurers, importers and exporters of goods and other like persons engaged in commerce and industry who frequently require the services of a Notary Public and in support of [his] [her] application to be appointed a Notary Public your Petitioner has obtained and filed in the Supreme Court Office a Certificate of Fitness signed by persons representative of the local business community together with a Certificate of Fitness signed by six Solicitors vouching your Petitioner's fitness and trustworthiness.

5. Your Petitioner is familiar with the law and practice relating to the administration of oaths and the taking of statutory declarations and affirmations and is competent to conduct notarial business in the English and Irish languages [and also in the _____ language(s) if so required.][3]
6. Your Petitioner has available a public office at [4] _____ wherein notarial business may be conducted in private and your Petitioner has no present intention of leaving the area for which [he] [she] seeks to be appointed.
7. If your Petitioner is appointed a Notary Public such appointment will be to the advantage and convenience of the legal, professional and business community in the area for which Petitioner seeks to be appointed.
8. If appointed a Notary Public, your Petitioner will give an appropriate Undertaking to observe the Code of Conduct for Notaries Public adopted by The Faculty of Notaries Public in Ireland on 21 November, 1986 and such rules, regulations and bye-laws governing the professional practice and procedure of Notaries Public in Ireland and the standards to be observed by them as shall from time to time be made and published by The Faculty of Notaries Public in Ireland.

MAY IT PLEASE THE CHIEF JUSTICE to appoint your Petitioner a Notary Public for[5]

Dated this _____ day of _____ 200

(Signed) A.B
Petitioner

Filed etc.,

Notes
[1]Law Term in which admitted
[2]Positions held since admission
[3]Foreign languages (if any); otherwise delete
[4]Address of public office
[5]Area for which Petitioner seeks appointment. If Dublin, insert 'the City of Dublin and the administrative counties of South Dublin, Fingal and Dunlaoghaire-Rathdown'.

APPENDIX 2A

THE CHIEF JUSTICE

IN THE MATTER OF A.B., A SOLICITOR, SEEKING TO BE APPOINTED A NOTARY PUBLIC
AND
IN THE MATTER OF THE COURTS (SUPPLEMENTAL PROVISIONS) ACT, 1961

AFFIDAVIT VERIFYING PETITION

I, A.B. of _____ in the City/County of _____
Solicitor, MAKE OATH and say as follows:

1. I am the Petitioner named in the above entitled matter.
2. So much of the said Petition as relates to me or to my own acts and deeds is true and so much of the said Petition as relates to the acts and deeds of any and every other person mentioned therein I believe to be true.
3. In accordance with the Practice Direction of the Chief Justice made on 28th day of March, 1994 pursuant to Order 127 of the Rules of the Superior Courts (No. 2) of 1993, I have obtained and exhibit herein a Certificate of Competency issued by The Faculty of Notaries Public in Ireland dated the ___ day of _____ 200_ upon which marked 'A' I have endorsed my name prior to the swearing of this Affidavit.
4. In support of the said Petition I exhibit a Certificate of Fitness signed by Solicitors upon which marked 'B' I have endorsed my name prior to the swearing of this Affidavit.
5. In further support of the said Petition I exhibit a Certificate of Fitness signed by members of the local business community upon which marked 'C' I have endorsed my name prior to the swearing of this Affidavit.
6. I depose as to the matters aforesaid of my own knowledge save where otherwise stated and where so stated I believe the same to be true.

SWORN this ___ day of _____ 200_
at _____ in the City/County of _____
before me a Commissioner for Oaths/Practising
Solicitor and I know the deponent

_____
Commissioner for Oaths/Practising Solicitor

APPENDIX 2B

THE CHIEF JUSTICE

IN THE MATTER OF A.B. [SOLICITOR] SEEKING TO BE APPOINTED A NOTARY PUBLIC

-AND-

IN THE MATTER OF THE COURTS (SUPPLEMENTAL PROVISIONS) ACT, 1961

CERTIFICATE OF FITNESS
(Solicitors)

We, the undersigned Solicitors, whose names and places of business are hereto subscribed DO HEREBY CERTIFY to the Chief Justice that A.B. a [Solicitor] of _____ in the City/County of _____ is, in our opinion, a person well suited and qualified by [his] [her] skill and trustworthiness to be constituted and appointed a Notary Public.

NAME   DESCRIPTION   ADDRESS

APPENDIX 2C

THE CHIEF JUSTICE

IN THE MATTER OF A.B. [SOLICITOR] SEEKING TO BE APPOINTED A NOTARY PUBLIC
AND
IN THE MATTER OF THE COURTS (SUPPLEMENTAL PROVISIONS) ACT, 1961

CERTIFICATE OF FITNESS
(Local Business Persons)

We, the undersigned, whose names, descriptions and places of residence or business are hereto subscribed DO HEREBY CERTIFY to the Chief Justice that A.B. a [Solicitor] of _____ in the City/County of _____ is, in our opinion, a person well suited and qualified by [his] [her] skill and trustworthiness to be constituted and appointed a Notary Public [and that such appointment, if made, would benefit the conduct of trade and commerce in the area in which we carry on business.][1]

NAME   DESCRIPTION   ADDRESS

---

[1] This statement is optional

APPENDIX 2D

THE CHIEF JUSTICE

IN THE MATTER OF A.B., A SOLICITOR, SEEKING TO BE APPOINTED A NOTARY PUBLIC

AND

IN THE MATTER OF THE COURTS (SUPPLEMENTAL PROVISIONS) ACT, 1961

NOTICE OF MOTION

TAKE NOTICE that on the _____ day of _____ 200__ at 10.30 in the forenoon, or on the first opportunity thereafter, Counsel on behalf of the Petitioner A.B. of _____ in the City/County of _____ will make application to the Chief Justice to constitute and appoint A.B. a Notary Public for _____[1]
WHICH SAID APPLICATION will be grounded on the Petition of the said A.B., the Affidavit verifying the said Petition, the Certificates of Fitness filed herein, the Certificate of Competency issued by the Faculty of Notaries Public in Ireland filed herein, the nature of the case and the reasons to be offered.

Dated this _____ day of _____ 200__

Signed: C.D. & Co.,
Solicitors for Petitioner
(Address)

To:
The Registrar,
The Supreme Court,
Four Courts,
Dublin 7

The Registrar,
The Faculty of Notaries Public in Ireland
34 Upper Baggot Street,
Dublin 4

The Secretary,
The Law Society of Ireland,
Blackhall Place,
Dublin 7

And to the undermentioned Notaries Public practising in the County for which Petitioner seeks to be appointed a Notary Public[2]

Notes:
[1]Insert place i.e. County or City and County for which Petitioner seeks to be appointed. Where Dublin, it should be described as 'The City of Dublin and the administrative counties of South Dublin, Fingal and Dunlaoghaire-Rathdown'.
[2]It is no longer required that the Notice of Motion be addressed to Notaries Public in adjoining counties.

APPENDIX 2E

DIRECTION

APPOINTMENT OF NOTARIES PUBLIC

In pursuance of the powers vested in me by Order 127 of the Rules of the Superior Courts (No. 2) of 1993 I hereby make the following direction and regulation concerning applications of persons to be appointed a Notary Public:

1. In an application to be appointed a Notary Public the Petitioner shall not be required to establish that the existing number of Notaries available for the transaction of notarial matters in the County, City, or district for which appointment is sought is inadequate to meet the needs of business and commerce and no averment as to such matter shall be necessary in the Petition or supporting documents.
2. This Direction shall take effect on and from January 26th 2006.

John L. Murray
CHIEF JUSTICE
25th January, 2006

APPENDIX 2F

APPOINTMENT BY CHIEF JUSTICE OF NOTARIES PUBLIC

PRACTICE DIRECTION

In pursuance of the powers vested in me by Order 127 of the Rules of the Superior Courts (No. 2 of 1993) I hereby make the following direction and regulation concerning the appointment of Notaries Public:

1. In an application to be appointed a Notary Public the Petitioner shall give an appropriate undertaking to observe the Code of Conduct for Notaries Public adopted by the Faculty of Notaries Public in Ireland on 21 November, 1986 and such rules, regulations and by-laws governing the professional practice and procedure of Notaries Public in Ireland and the standards to be observed by them as shall from time to time be made and published by the Faculty of Notaries Public in Ireland.
2. This Direction shall take effect on and from October 2nd 2006.

John L. Murray
CHIEF JUSTICE
20th September 2006

APPENDIX 3

TRANSLATOR'S AFFIDAVIT

I, A.B. of _____ in the [City] [County] of _____, aged 18 years and upwards, professional translator, MAKE OATH and say as follows:

1. I am proficient and competent in the use of the _____[1] language in which the annexed document marked 'A' is written.
2. I am proficient and competent in the use of the English language in which the annexed document marked 'B' is written.
3. My knowledge of and proficiency and competency in the _____[1] language has been obtained as a result of[2] _____ and my knowledge of and proficiency and competency in the English language derives from my having been educated in [Ireland] [England] through the medium of English to advanced level.
4. I am competent and well qualified to translate documents of a legal and commercial nature from the _____[1] language into the English language.
5. The document in the English language annexed hereto marked 'B', which has been prepared by me, is a true and fair translation into English of the document in the _____[1] language annexed hereto marked 'A' upon each of which documents I have endorsed my name for the purposes of identification prior to swearing this affidavit.

SWORN by the said A.B. at _____
in the [City] [County] of _____
before me C.D.[3] _____ [and I
know the deponent][4] [the said A.B. having
been identified to me by [his] [her] Passport
No. _____ issued at _____
and currently in force.]

(Sgd.) C.D.
Notary Public/Commissioner for Oaths/Practising Solicitor

Notes
[1] Identify the foreign language e.g. French, Italian, Hungarian etc.
[2] Insert relevant information as to means of knowledge and competency.
[3] Insert 'notary public, commissioner for oaths or practicing solicitor', as case may be.
[4] If the person taking the Affidavit does not know deponent, the statement as to knowing deponent should be deleted and the words following in parenthesis used with the parenthesis removed.

APPENDIX 3A

STATUTORY DECLARATION OF TRANSLATOR

I, A.B., of _____ in the [City] [County] of _____ aged 18 years and upwards   DO SOLEMNLY AND SINCERELY DECLARE that:

1. I am proficient and competent in the use of the _____[1] language in which the annexed document marked 'A' is written.

2. I am proficient and competent in the use of the English language in which the annexed document marked 'B' is written.

3. My knowledge of and proficiency and competency in the _____[1] language has been obtained as a result of [2]_____ and my knowledge of and proficiency and competence in the English language derives from my having been educated in [Ireland] [England] through the medium of English to advanced level.

4. I am competent and well qualified to translate documents of a legal and commercial nature from the _____[1] language into the English language.

5. The document in the English language annexed hereto marked 'B', which has been prepared by me, is a true and fair translation into English of the document in the _____[1] language annexed hereto marked 'A' upon each of which documents I have endorsed my name for the purposes of identification prior to the making of this declaration.

And I make this solemn declaration conscientiously believing the same to be true and by virtue of the Statutory Declarations Act, 1938.

(signed) A.B.

Declared before me C.D., [Notary Public/Commissioner for Oaths/ Practising solicitor] by A.B. [who is personally known to me] or [who is identified to me by E.F. who is personally known to me] or [whose identity has been established to me before the taking of this declaration in accordance with section 2 of the Statutory Declarations Act, 1938 (as amended)][3] at _____ in the [City] [County] of _____ on this ___ day of _____ 200 .

(signed) C.D.
Notary Public[3]

Notes

[1] Identify the foreign language e.g. French, Italian, Hungarian etc.
[2] Insert relevant information as to means of knowledge and competence
[3] Insert means of identification of declarant if no personal knowledge.

At the time of writing, the Civil Law (Miscellaneous Provisions) Bill, 2006 upon which the form of declaratory words used above is based, has not been enacted.

APPENDIX 4

ACKNOWLEDGEMENT AND CONFIRMATION RELATING TO THE EXECUTION AND NOTARISING OF A FOREIGN POWER OF ATTORNEY

To:

(Name of Notary Public)

I, the undersigned, hereby state as follows -

1. I am in the process of purchasing/selling/mortgaging a property in _____

2. I appear before you in your capacity as Notary Public to have you witness my signature to a Power of Attorney (the 'Document') appointing a foreign Attorney (or Attornies) to act for me in connection with the above mentioned transaction and in that capacity to execute and sign documents on my behalf and otherwise to do all such matters as are set out in the Document.

3. I understand the purpose and nature of the Document which, before I came to you, was carefully explained to me by a person whom I trust.

4. For the purpose of record, I acknowledge and confirm that:

    (a) I have identified myself to you me by reference to my Passport No _____ issued at _____ and a utility bill in my name providing my current address.
    (b) my purpose in coming before you is to have you, as a Notary Public, witness my signature to the Document;
    (c) you did not draw up the Document:
    (d) you are not my legal adviser and you have not been asked to provide, nor have you offered to give, legal or other ad-

vice regarding the transaction or the Document other than the recommendation in (f) below;

(e) you told me that you are not competent in the foreign language in which the Document is drawn up/partly drawn up, nor in the laws of the country or state where the document is to be received and acted upon;

(f) you did tell me that Powers of Attorney are important legal documents that could have potentially serious legal and financial consequences for persons signing them; and for that reason I should obtain competent legal, financial and taxation advice on the implications of signing the Document;

(g) you told me that I was free to get legal advice also in relation to signing this Acknowledgement and Confirmation.

5. I have read this Acknowledgement and Confirmation and accept that it has been drawn up in non-technical language which I fully understand.

Dated this _____ day of _____ 200

Signed:_____

APPENDIX 5

ACKNOWLEDGEMENT AND CONFIRMATION RELATING TO THE EXECUTION AND NOTARISING OF FOREIGN POWER OF ATTORNEY

To:
(Name of Notary Public)

We, the undersigned, hereby state as follows -

1. We are in the process of purchasing/selling/mortgaging a property in _____

2. We appear before you in your capacity as Notary Public to have you witness our signatures to a Power of Attorney (the 'Document') appointing a foreign Attorney (or Attornies) to act for us in connection with the above mentioned transaction and in that capacity to execute and sign documents on our behalf and otherwise to do all such matters as are set out in the Document.

3. We understand the purpose and nature of the Document which, before coming to you, was carefully explained to us by a person whom we trust.

4. For the purpose of record we acknowledge and confirm that:

    (a) we have identified ourselves to you by reference to our Passports No _____ and No _____ issued at _____ and also a utility bill providing our current address;
    (b) our purpose in coming before you is to have you, as a Notary Public, witness our signatures to the Document;
    (c) you did not draw up the Document;
    (d) you are not our legal adviser and you have not been asked to provide, nor have you offered to give, legal or other

advice regarding the transaction or the Document other than the recommendation in (f) below;

(e) you told us that you are not competent in the foreign language in which the Document has been drawn up/partly drawn up, nor in the laws of the country or state where the document is to be received and acted upon;

(f) you told us that Powers of Attorney are important legal documents that could have potentially serious legal and financial consequences for persons signing them; and, for that reason, we should obtain competent legal, financial and taxation advice on the implications of signing the Document;

(g) you told us that we were free to get legal advice also in relation to signing this Acknowledgement and Confirmation.

5. We have read this Acknowledgement and Confirmation and accept that it has been drawn up in non-technical language which each of us fully understands.

Dated this _____ day of _____ 200

Signed:_____

APPENDIX 6

NOTARIAL CERTIFICATE VERIFYING A COPY OF THE TESTAMUR OF A DEGREE, DIPLOMA, CERTIFICATE OR OTHER QUALIFICATION

TO ALL TO WHOM THESE PRESENTS SHALL COME, I A.B., Notary Public, duly constituted and appointed and practising at [1]_____ SEND GREETINGS AND HEREBY DECLARE AND CERTIFY as follows:

1. There has been produced to me a document described as the testamur of a [Degree of _____ [2]] [Diploma in _____ [2]] [Certificate in _____ [2]] ('the testamur') appearing to have been conferred on or granted to C.D. by [3]_____.

2. The document annexed hereto which purports to be a copy of the testamur has been compared by me with the testamur and is a true and faithful copy thereof.

IN FAITH AND TESTIMONY whereof I, the aforementioned Notary Public, have hereunto signed my name and affixed my official seal at [4]_____ on this ____ day of _____ 200

(signed) A.B.
Notary Public
(address)
Commissioned for Life

[1] Address of public office
[2] Describe the degree, diploma or qualification
[3] Name of University or College
[4] Place at which seal affixed

APPENDIX 7

SHORT FORM OF NOTARIAL CERTIFICATE OF DUE EXECUTION OF A DEED e.g.. POWER OF ATTORNEY, BY A COMPANY

NOTARIAL CERTIFICATE

On the _____ day of _____ 200 at _____ in the [City] [County] of

BEFORE ME

A.B. Notary Public, duly constituted and appointed, and practising at _____ in the City/County of

APPEARED

C.D. to me [personally known] [identified by reference to Passport No. _____ issued at _____], who

DECLARED

that he/she is the Secretary/Director of E.F Limited/PLC, the company that executed the annexed document; that he/she knows the official seal of the Company; that the seal affixed to the said document is the official seal of the company; that the seal was affixed by authority of the Board of Directors and in accordance with the Articles of Association of the Company, and that the said C.D., and G.H. by like authority subscribed their names to the said document opposite the seal as part of the Company's sealing regulation.

CERTIFIED by me, the said A.B. Notary Public, at _____ in the City/County of _____ within the jurisdiction for which I am appointed, on the _____ day of _____ 200

(Sgd.) A.B.
Notary Public   L.S.
(address)
Commissioned for Life

APPENDIX 8

FORM OF STATUTORY DECLARATION

I, A.B., do solemnly and sincerely declare that [*here insert text of matter to be declared*] and I make this solemn declaration conscientiously believing the same to be true and by virtue of the Statutory Declarations Act, 1938.

[Signed] A.B.

Declared before me _____ [*name in capitals*] a [Notary Public] [Commissioner for Oaths] [Peace Commissioner] [person authorised by [*insert authorising statutory provision*] _____ to take and receive statutory declarations] by A.B.

[who is personally known to me],

or

[who is identified to me by C.D. who is personally known to me]

or

[whose identity has been established to me before the taking of this Declaration by the production to me of

> passport no. [*passport number*] issued on [*date of issue*] by the authorities of [*issuing state*], which is an authority recognised by the Irish Government]

or

> national identity card no. [*identity card number*] issued on [*date of issue*] by the authorities of [*issuing state*] [which is an EU Member State, the Swiss Confederation or a Contracting Party to the EEA Agreement]

or

aliens passport no. (*document equivalent to a passport*) [*passport number*] issued on [*date of issue*] by the authorities of [issuing state] which is an authority recognised by the Irish Government]

or

refugee travel document no. [*document number*] issued on [*date of issue*] by the Minister for Justice, Equality and Law Reform]

or

travel document (other than refugee travel document) [*document no.*] issued on [*date of issue*] by the Minister for Justice, Equality and Law Reform]

At _____ [*place of signature*] this _____ day of _____ [*date*]

[*signature of witness*]'.

Note:

This form of Statutory Declaration is set out in Section 61 of the Civil Law (Miscellaneous Provisions) Bill 2006 as presented on 20 April 2006 but not enacted at the time of writing.

APPENDIX 9

NOTARIAL CERTIFICATE VERIFYING DOCUMENTS FOR FOREIGN ADOPTION

TO ALL TO WHOM THESE PRESENTS SHALL COME

I, A.B. Notary Public, duly constituted and appointed for the [City] [County] of _____ [and the adjoining Counties of _____ and _____] Ireland and practising at _____ in the [City] [County] of _____ Ireland,

DO HEREBY CERTIFY as follows:

1. That the documents hereunto annexed and described in the Schedule hereto and therein numbered 1 to [ ] inclusive, ground the application to the adoption authorities of _____ by C.D. (male spouse) and E.F. (female spouse), Irish citizens resident in Ireland, to adopt a child of _____ aforesaid.

2. That such of the documents enumerated in the Schedule as are described as originals bear all the signs of authenticity required by Irish law and, in my opinion, are the true originals; and that such of the documents described in the Schedule as copies of original documents (that have been retained) have been carefully examined by me and compared with such originals and, in my opinion, are true, faithful and complete copies of such originals.

3. That for the purpose of identification and authentication, I have numbered each of the aforementioned documents and have signed my name and affixed my official seal thereto and on the cover page attached to such documents.

IN FAITH AND TESTIMONY whereof I, the said A.B., Notary Public, have hereunto subscribed my name and affixed my official seal of office at _____ in the [City] [County] of _____ on this _____ day of _____ 200

A.B.
Notary Public
(address)   L.S.
Commissioned for Life

SCHEDULE

1. Adoption Board Certificate of Eligibility and Suitability.
2. Health Service Executive Home Study Adoption Social Report.
3. Immigration Clearance Letter.
4. Marriage Certificate (Civil) of Applicants.
5. Birth Certificate (husband)
6. Birth Certificate (wife)
7. Copy Passport (husband)
8. Copy Passport (wife).
9. Garda/Police Clearance Letter (husband)
10. Garda/Police Clearance Letter (wife)
11. Medical Certificate verifying Physical and Mental Health (husband)
12. Medical Certificate verifying Physical and Mental Health (Wife)
13. Medical Certificate verifying Infertility.
14. Occupation/Income Certificate (husband)
15. Occupation/Income Certificate (wife)
16. Health Service Executive Undertaking to Continue Supervision.
17. Irish Adoption Board Letter of Introduction.
18. Irish Adoption Board Certificate of Recognition of Adoption from Donor Country.
19. Certificate of Valuation of Assets.
20. (Any other document that might be requested)

TABLE OF STATUTES

E = England
NI = Northern Ireland

A

Adoption Act, 1952 (No. 25 of 1952) 57-59
Adoption Act, 1991 (No. 14 of 1991) 58-59
Adoption Act, 1998 (No. 10 of 1998) 59

B

Banking and Financial Dealings Act, 1971
    (E) C 80 40
Bank Holidays Act, 1871 (34 & 35 Vict. c. 17) 41
Bills of Exchange Act, 1882 (45 & Vic. c. 61) 40

C

Central Bank Act, 1989 (No. 16 of 1989) 40-41
Cheques Act, 1959 (No. 19 of 1959) 41
Companies Act, 1963 (No. 33 of 1963) 51
Companies Act, (Northern Ireland) 1960 (NI) 53
Competition Act, 2002 (No. 14 of 2002) 16
Conveyancing Act, 1881 (44 & 45 Vict. c. 41) 26-29
Conveyancing Act, 1882 (45 & 46 Vict. c. 39) 26-29
Criminal Justice Act, 1994 (No. 15 of 1994) 65
Criminal Justice (Theft and Fraud) Act, 2001
    (No. 50 of 2001) 69

D

Diplomatic and Consular Officers (Provision of Services)
    Act, 1993 (No. 33 of 1993) 25

E

Electronic Commerce Act, 2000 (No. 27 of 2000)............72,74,75

F

Family Law (Divorce) Act, 1996 (No. 33 of 1996)...............30
Family Law (Miscellaneous Provisions) Act, 1997
   (No. 18 of 1997)..29-30

I

Investment Funds, Companies and Miscellaneous
   Provisions Act, 2006 (No. 41 of 2006).......................25

P

Powers of Attorney Act, 1996 (No. 12 of 1996)................26-32

R

Refugee Act, 1996 (No. 17 of 1996)..................................10,23

S

Settled Land Act 1882 (44 & 45 Vict. c. 38).........................27
Statute of Frauds (Ireland) 1695 (7 Will. 3 c. 12)................74
Statutory Declarations Act, 1938 (No. 37 of 1938).............22,92,100
Stock Exchange Act, 1995 (No. 9 of 1995).........................30

EU DIRECTIVES

European Signatures Directive (Directive on a
   Community Framework for Electronic Signature)
   (1999/93/EC)...72
Electronic Commerce Directive (2000/31/EC) 72
Prevention of the use of the financial systems for the
   purpose of money laundering

First Directive 91/308/EEC 65-66
Second Directive 2001/97/EEC 66
Third Directive 2005/60/EEC 66

STATUTORY INSTRUMENTS

Companies (Forms) Order, 1964 (S.I. No. 45 of 1964) 51-52
Companies (Forms) (Amendment) Order, 1999
   (S.I. No. 14 of 1999) 51-52
Criminal Justice Act, 1994 (Section 32) Regulations
   of 2003 (S.I. No. 242 of 2003) 65-66
Enduring Powers of Attorney Regulations, 1996
   (S.I. No. 196 of 1996) 31-32
Enduring Powers of Attorney (Personal Care Decisions)
   Regulations, 1996 (S.I. No. 287 of 1996) 31
Enduring Powers of Attorney (Northern Ireland) Order, 1987
   (S.I. No. 1627 of 1987) NI 33
Enduring Powers of Attorney (Northern Ireland
   Consequential Amendment) Order, 1987
   (S.I. No. 1628 of 1987) NI 33
European Communities (Companies) Regulations, 1973
   (S.I. No. 163 of 1973) 53
Rules of the Superior Courts (No. 2) of 1993
   (S.I. No. 265 of 1993) 2,6,49-51
Rules of the Superior Courts (No. 1), Proof of Foreign
   Diplomatic, Consular and Public Documents, 1999
   (S.I. No. 3 of 1999) 49

BILLS

Civil Law (Miscellaneous Provisions) Bill, 2006
   (No. 20 of 2006) 22

INDEX

A

Abolition of Legalisation,
    under Hague Convention of 5 October 1961, 1, 42-52
    under EC Convention of 25 May 1987, 1, 42, 44-52
    under EC Convention of June 1968, 48-50, 52

Absentia,
    documents signed in, 14-15

Accoutrements of Notary, stamps, 17-19

Acknowledgement,
    of appearer's understanding of document, 18
    for use with foreign power of attorney, form of, 13-14, 94-97

Acknowledgements,
    of Authors, xi

Act,
    Notarial, 3-5
    Public, 5
    Acte probant sese ipsa, 42

Adoption,
    foreign or inter-country, 2, 57-64
    legalisation, 57-60

Administration of oaths etc., 24-25

Advanced Electronic Signature, 73

Affidavit,
    verifying petition, 83
    of translator, 13, 90

Affirmation,
    form of words of, 24

Ahern, Dermot C. T.D.,
    Minister for Foreign Affairs, 23

Albania, 55

American Samoa, 55

Andorra, 55

Angola, 55

Anguilla, 55

Antigua and Barbuda, 55

Appearer(s),
    identification of etc., 10-11, 14, 67-68

Application,
    for appointment as notary, public 2, 6-7, 9, 78-89

Appointment with Notary,
    preparation for, 62

Apostille,
    definition, 45
    contents, 46
    form of certificate, 54
    Hague Convention of 5 October 1961, 1, 42-54

Argentina, 55

Armenia, 55

Aruba, 55

Association of Chartered Accountants,
    Recommendation re Foreign Property Acquisition, 12-13

Attestation, 12, 14-16, 67

Attorney,
    Power of, 26-30

Enduring Power of, 2, 26, 30-33
foreign lawyer as, 11
Australia, 55
Austria, 55
Authentication,
of document by notary, 67
Authors, vii
Azerbaijan, 55
Azores, 55

B

Bahamas, 55
Bank Holidays Act, 1871, 40
Banking and Financial Dealings, Act, 1971, 40
Barbados, 55
Belarus, 55
Belgium, 55
Belize, 55
Bermuda, 55
Bill,
utility, production of to establish identity, 10, 62, 67
Bills of Exchange
days of grace, abolition of, 1, 40
falling due on Saturday, Sunday or Bank Holiday, 40
noting, 66
presentment on a Saturday, 41
protesting, 66
time of payment, 41
Bosnia and Herzegovina, 55
Botswana, 55
British Antartic Territory, 55

British Virgin Islands, 55
Brooke's Notary,
Treatise on the office of
a Notary of England, 3
Brunei Darussalam, 55
Bulgaria, 55

C

Capacity
legal, 18, 30
notary to vouch, 10-11, 18
Care
notary's duty of, 11, 12
Cayman Islands, 55
Central Bank Act, 1989, 40-41
Certificate,
Apostille, 1, 45-50, 54
of competency to be notary public, 6-8, 80-81
criteria for, 6-8
of fitness, 9
of due execution, of power of attorney, 99
Certification,
of copy document as a true copy 17-18
Central Office,
registration of Power of Attorney, 30
registration of Enduring Power of Attorney, 32
issue of Special Summons to register Enduring Power of Attorney, 32
Cheques Act, 1959, 41
Chief Justice,
appointment of notaries

public, 9
direction of,
 re certificate of
  competency, 6-7
 dispensing with requirement
  to show need, 9
 Foreword of, (ix)
 powers conferred on by
  Order 127 Rules of the
  Superior Courts, 6-7
Child,
 adoption of foreign, 57-64
 notice to, of execution of
  Enduring Power of
  Attorney, 31
Christmas Day,
 bill falling due on, 40
Columbia, 55
Companies Act, 1963, 51-53
Company,
 European Communities
  (Companies) Regulations,
  1973, 53
 giving Power of Attorney, 53
 registration of attorney's name
  in Companies Registration
  Office, 53
Companies (Forms) (Amendment)
 Order, 1999, 51-52
Competent knowledge,
 of foreign language, 14
 of notarial matters by
  applicant, 6-7
Conduct,
 of notary public, 10-16
Conflict of interest, 11
Consular Services,
 Department of Foreign
  Affairs, 46-49
Conventions,
 Abolishing Requirement of
  Legalisation for Foreign
  Public Documents of 5
  October 1961 (Hague
  Convention), 1, 42-52
 Abolishing the Legalisation of
  Documents in the
  Member States of the
  European Communities
  of 25
  May 1987 (EC
  Convention of 1987), 1,
  42, 44-52
 Abolishing Legalisation of
  Documents Executed by
  Diplomatic Agents or
  Consular Officers of June
  1968, 48-50, 52
Croatia, 55
Cybernotarial Ireland Ltd., 71
Cyprus, 55
Czech Republic, 55

D

Data,
 in electronic form, 73
Dating of,
 notarial act, 4-5
Days of Grace, 1, 40
Death,
 revokes Power of Attorney,
  27, 29
Declaration,
 amendment to Statutory

Declarations Act, 1938,
    22-23
Civil Law (Miscellaneous
    Provisions) Bill, 2006,
    22-23
means of establishing
    identity under, 22-24
used for Ship Protest, 34
words for verbal, 24
Declarant, 22, 24-25
    unable to read, 25
Deeds,
    execution of, by donor of
        Power of Attorney, 28
    best practice re, 28
Degrees,
    certifying copies of, 16
Denmark,
    signatory to EC Convention
        of 25 May 1987, 49
Department of Foreign Affairs,
    'competent authority' for the
        purposes of the Hague
        Convention of 5 October
        1961, 45
    'central authority' for the
        purposes of the EC
        Convention of 25 May
        1987, 49
Deposit,
    of Power of Attorney in
        Central Office, 30
    of Enduring Power of
        Attorney in Wards of
        Court Office, 32
Designated,
    country,
        under Criminal Justice

Act, 1994, 68-69
    person, 66
    solicitor as, 66
Developers,
    of foreign properties, 11
Digital Image, 24
Diplomas,
    certifying, 16
Diplomatic Agent, 43-44, 48, 50
Direction,
    of donor of power of attorney,
        26
    instrument signed by, 26, 28
    practice re registration of
        Enduring Power of
        Attorney, 32
Direction(s),
    by Chief Justice (see under
        Chief Justice)
Disclaimer (see
Acknowledgment)
Djibouti, 55
Documentary Proofs in Adoption,
    60-63
Documents,
    foreign language, 11-14
    pages not bound together,
        15-16
    public, 5, 42, 44-49
    used for identification, 10,
        22-23, 62, 67
Dominica, 55
Donee,
    of Power of Attorney, 27
    of Enduring Power of
        Attorney, 30
    protection of, 29
Donegan, James, 34-35

Donor,
   of Power of Attorney, 26-29
   of Enduring Power of
      Attorney, 30
   execution of Power of
      Attorney by, 28-29, 31
Donor's spouse
   notice re Enduring Power of
      Attorney, 31
Dossier,
   contents of, in foreign
      adoption application,
      59-61, 63
Double Taxation, 12-13
Driving Licence,
   used for identification, 67
   not generally acceptable, 10,
      23
Duty of Care of Notary,
   as service provider, 12
   dealing with foreign
      language documents,
      11-13
   dealing with foreign adoption
      document, 62
   under common law, 11

E

Ecuador, 55
European Economic Agreement
   (EEA) 23, 100
E-Commerce,
   UNICTRAL Model Law on,
      72
EC Convention of 25 May 1987,
   1, 42, 44, 48-52

Electronic Attestation, 75-76
   defined, 73
Electronic Contract, 73
Electronic Commerce, 2, 71-72,
   74
Electronic Commerce Act, 2000,
   72-75
Electronic Commerce Directive
   (2000/31/EC), 72
Electronic Funds Transfers,
   in money laundering, 65
Electronic Signature,
   advanced, 73
   defined, 73
Element(s),
   of notarial act, 4-5
   foreign, 10
Eligibility,
   adoption, 59
   certificate of, 60
   declaration, 59
El Salvador, 55
Enduring Power of Attorney,
   (EPA), 2, 26, 30-33 and
   (see Powers of Attorney
      Act, 1999 *post)*
Enduring Powers of Attorney:
   Guidelines for Solicitors
      (2004), 32
Enduring Powers of Attorney
   (Northern Ireland) Order,
      1987, 33
Enduring Powers of Attorney
   (Northern Ireland
   Consequential
   Amendment) Order,
      1987, 33
England, 3

English Language,
　translation 13-14, 18
E-Passport, 23-24
Estonia, 55
Ethics, 7
European Communities
　(Companies) Regulations,
　1973, 53
European Economic Area, 10, 23,
　100
European Signatures Directive,
　(1999/93/EC), 72
European Union (see Foreword),
　ix
Evidence,
　driving licence, 10
　of identification, 10
　passport as, 62
Exercise of Notary's Function,
　duties of notary, 10-16, 68
　standard of care, 4, 11-12
Ex Tenebras Lux, 20

F

Faculty,
　of Notaries Public in Ireland,
　　1, 6, 8-9, 13-14, 22, 25,
　　34, 70
　Examination Body of, 7
　Examination,
　　to obtain certificate of
　　　competency, 7
Faith,
　public, in notarial act, 3-4
Falkland Islands, 55
Family,
　history in adoption, 60-61

Family Law (Divorce) Act, 1996,
　30
Family Law (Miscellaneous
　Provisions) Act, 1997, 29-30
Fees,
　adoption applications, 64
　generally, 64
　notarial, 16
Fellow of the Institute of Bankers
　(see Authors)
Fiji, 55
Financial Action Task Force
　(FATF), 68-69
Financial affairs,
　in adoption, 60-62
Finland, 55
Fitness,
　certificates of, 9, 84, 85
　applicant must file, 83
Foreign,
　adoption, 2, 8, 57-64
　developers, 11
　estate agents, 11
　language, 18
　property transaction, 11
　public documents, 5
　Power of Attorney, 11-14
　　translation, 13-14
Foreign Affairs, Department of,
　22, 43, 45-49
　Minister for, 23
Forgery, 16, 20
Formality,
　under Hague Convention,
　　44-46
France, 55
French Guyana (or Guiana), 55
Frauds, Statute of, (Ir.) 1695, 74

French,
  lawyers, 3
  language, 19
  notaire, 3
  word *actes*, 3
French Polynesia, 55
Functions,
  of notary public, 66

G

Gallagher, Brian, 28
Garda Síochána
  clearance letter, foreign
    adoption, 61, 103
  money-laundering, 66-68
Germany, 55
German Notar, 3
Gibraltar, 55
Gibson, William, 71
Good Friday,
  bill falling due on, 40
Government (Irish), 23
Grace,
  days of, 1, 40
Granada, 55
Greece, 55
Griffin, Gerard F.
  (see Acknowledgements)
Guadeloupe, 55
Guam, 55
Guernsey, 55
Guidelines, Law Society,
  money laundering legislation,
    69-70
Guyana, 55

H

Hague Convention of 5 October
  1961,
  general, 1, 5, 42-49,
    51-54, 63
  public documents, 1, 5, 42-49,
    51-54
Health Service Executive,
  foreign adoption certificate,
    59-61, 103
High Court,
  Central office, deposit of
    Power of Attorney in, 30
  Wards of Court office,
    registration of Enduring
    Power of Attorney,
      32
  powers of court in
    relation to, 32
History,
  of notary public, part of
    examination syllabus, 7
Home Study Programme,
  foreign adoption certificate,
    59-60, 103
Honduras, 55
Hong Kong, 55
Hungary, 55

I

Iceland, 55
Identity, 10
  proof of, 10
  national identity card, 10, 23
  driving licence, 10, 23, 67

passport, 10, 23, 67
utility bill, 10, 67
travel document, 10, 23, 101
money laundering, 67
Immigration,
certificate, 60
clearance letter, foreign
adoption, 60, 103
In Absentia, Attestation,
breach of duty, 14-15
disciplinary action, 15
Incapacity,
see under Power of Attorney,
India, 55
Inter-Country Adoptions, 67-64
International,
see under European
Communities
European Union, 10, 12, 23,
68-69
International Law,
part of examination syllabus,
7, 36
Introduction
letter of, in adoption, 61
in money laundering
prevention, 67
Investor,
person purchasing property
abroad, 11-14
Ireland, 55, 58, 69
double taxation agreements,
12-13
maritime nation, 34
Hague Conference on Private
International Law, 42, 75
Irish Adoption Board,
documents for foreign
adoption, 50, 60-61,
102-103
Irish Citizen,
property acquisition by, 11-13
Irish couples,
in adoption 57, 58, 65
Isle of Man, 55
Israel, 55
Italy, 55
Italian phrase for 'signed
before me' in, 19

J

Japan, 55
Jersey, 55
Justice,
Minister for Justice, Equality
and Law Reform, 22, 23
statutory declarations, 22,
100-101
regulations governing
Enduring Powers of
Attorney, 30-31

K

Kazakhstan, 55
Keeping of Records by Notary,
34, 36, 65-66, 68-69
Kelly, Kathy
(see Acknowledgements)
Kidd, 30
Kiribati (Gilbert Islands), 55
Knowledge (Notary's),
of declarant of statutory
declaration, 22, 100
of financial or taxation,

position of appearer,
  11-14
of foreign language, 12-14
of foreign law, 12-14
Koran, 25

L

Language,
  foreign, 12-14
  document in, 12-14
  certified translation of, 13,
    90-91
  translator's affidavit, 90-91
  translator's declaration,
    92-93
Las Vegas,
  Conference on eNotarisation,
    75
Latin Notaries, 3, 75
Latvia, 55
Laundering,
  proceeds of crime (see
    Money-laundering)
Law Society of Ireland,
  Guidelines on Money-
    laundering, 69-70
Legal adviser,
  notary not acting as, 11-12,
    14, 94-95, 96-97
Legalisation, 1, 5, 42-45, 47-52, 63
Legal documents,
  structure of, 26
Lesotho, 55
Letter of Introduction
  (see under Foreign Adoption),
  (see also under Money-
    laundering),

Liberia, 55
Licence,
  driving, used for
    identification, 10, 23, 65
Liechtenstein, 55
Lithuania, 55
Log,
  ship's, 36, 38-39
  inspection of by notary, 36
London,
  Scriveners' Company of, 1
Lucas, 20
Luxembourg, 55

M

Macau (SAR), 55
Macedonia, 55
Madeira, 55
Maintain Records,
  notary to, 34, 36, 65-66,
    68-69
Malawi, 55
Malta, 55
Marriage Certificate,
  in foreign adoption dossier,
    60, 103
Marshall Islands, 55
Martinique, 55
Master,
  of ship or vessel, 34-38
  protest by, 34-38
Mauritius, 55
Mayotte (Fr. Department), 55
McCarthy Timothy Re, 6
Means of identification,
  (see under Identity)

Medical Certificate,
   in foreign adoption dossier, 61
Medical history,
   in foreign adoption, 61-62
Member Firm,
   under Stock Exchange Act, 29
Member State of European Union,
   identity card issued by, 10, 23
Memorandum & Articles of Association,
   authentication under Companies Act, 51-52
Mercantile Law, 7
Mexico, 56
Minister for Foreign Affairs, 23
Minister for Justice, Equality and Law Reform, 22, 23, 30
Monaco, 56
Money-laundering,
   name and shame policy, 69
Monserrat (UK Territory), 56
Mozambique, 56
Multipage document,
   notarising procedure, 15-16
Myanmar (former Burma), 69

N

Name of Appearer,
   on passport, 10, 62, 67
   on utility bill, 10, 62, 67
Name of Notary,
   to appear on official seal, 4
Name of Donor
   in conveyance under Power of Attorney, 28
Namibia, 56
Nationals, Foreign,
   identification of, 22
National Identity Card, 10, 23
Netherlands, 56
Netherlands Antilles, 56
New Caledonia, 56
New Zealand, 56
Nieu, 56
Non Co-operative Countries and Territories (NCCT), 69
Northern Ireland,
   Enduring Power of Attorney in, 32-33
Northern Mariana Islands, 56
Norway, 56
Notaire (Fr.), 3
Notar (Gm.), 3
Notarial Accoutrements, 17-20
Notarial Act,
   components of, 4-5
Notarial Attestation of Signature, 4, 10, 12, 14-15, 16, 18-19, 53
Notarial Certificate,
   in adoption 63
   of copy testamur of degree etc., 98
   of execution of Power of Attorney, 99
   verifying documents in foreign adoption 63, 102-103
Notarial Fees
   Competition Act, 2002, 16
   criteria for determining, 16, 64

not fixed, 16
not prescribed, 16
Notarial Forum of United
  Kingdom, 1
Notarial Services,
  fees, 16
  criteria for, 16, 64
Notarial Stamp (see under
  Notarial Accoutrements)
  for foreign language
  documents, 18
Notaries Public,
  Code of Conduct, 9, 81, 82
  Direction(s) of Chief
    Justice re, 2, 6, 9, 78, 79,
    88, 89
  knowledge of notarial
    matters by applicants, 6-8
  certificate of competency, 6,
    80
  dispensing with
    requirement of need, 9,
    88
  power of Chief Justice
    to make directions re, 2,
    6, 78
  regulations governing
    admission of, 2, 6, 78
  role in adoption, 62-63
  rules under Order 127 RSC,
    6-7, 78
Notario (Sp.), 3
Notary Profession
  entry standard, 6-8
Notary Public,
  application for appointment,
    2, 9
  attesting signature made

in absentia, 14-15
  conduct of, 2, 10-16
  duties of, as service provider,
    11-12
  not competent in foreign
    law (generally), 12, 14
  not competent in foreign
    language (generally),
    12, 14
  not legal adviser (generally),
    12, 14
  obligation to establish
    identity of appearer, 10,
    65
  official seal of, 5
  not privy to financial or
    taxation information of
    appearer (generally), 12
Notaries Society, 1
Note of Protest (Ship), 34-35, 37
Notice of Motion,
  on application for
    appointment as notary
    public, 9, 86-87
Noting,
  foreign bills of exchange, 40
  ship protest, 34-38

O

Oath(s),
  use of Qur'an when
    administering to
    Muslims, 25
  words of, when swearing
    affidavit, 24
Oporto,
  Agreement on the European

Economic Area signed
at, 10, 23
Order 127 RSC, 6-7, 78
Original document,
certification as, 17
certification as true copy of,
17
Overseas Companies, 51-52

P

Panama, 56
Paper based systems,
(see Electronic Commerce
Act, 2000)
Passports
biometric passports, 23-24
digitised form, 23-24
Paraphs, 20-21
Permanent Bureau
of the Hague Conference on
Private International Law,
46
Petition,
affidavit verifying petition
for appointment as a
notary public, 9, 83
Certificate of Fitness, 9
precedents of, 84, 85
Philippines,
bilateral agreement for
adoption, 63
Photographic Identification, 10,
24, 67
Poland, 56
Police Clearance Letter, 61, 103
Portugal, 56

Powers of Attorney,
corporations, 27-28
definition of, 26
irrevocable, if enduring, 32
structure of, 28
statutory format, 27
proof of, 29-30
purchaser of any estate or
interest in land, 30
regulations, 30-31
revocable on death, 27
Powers of Attorney Act, 1996, 2,
26
Practice Direction of Chief
Justice, 2, 6-7, 9, 78, 79, 88,
89
Practice Direction
re registration of Enduring
Power of Attorney, 32
Precedents,
Acknowledgement relating
to foreign Powers of
Attorney, 94-97
Affidavit verifying Petition
for appointment as
Notary Public, 83
Certificate(s) of Fitness,
84-85
Due Execution of Power of
Attorney by a company,
99
Notarial Certificate verifying
documents for foreign
adoption, 102-103
Notice of Motion, 86-87
Petition for appointment as
Notary Public, 81-82
Translator's affidavit, 90-91

Translator's Statutory
    Declaration, 92-93
Presentation of documents to
    Notary, 15
Principal work, 1-3, 10, 14, 17,
    20, 22, 25, 26, 34, 40, 51, 53,
    57
Private Acts, 3, 5
Private International Law, 7,
    42-43
Probate,
    Administration and Taxation
    Committee of the Law
    Society, 32
Promissory Notes, 1, 40
Proof of Identity, 10, 22-24, 62,
    65-69, 100-101
Protesting Bills of Exchange,
    40-41
Protests, Ships, 34-39
Public Acts, 3
Public Body,
    electronic certification, 75
    service provider, 75
Public documents, 5
    EC Convention of 25 May
        1987, 1, 42, 44-45
    Hague Convention of 5
        October 1961, 1, 42,
        44-45
Publica Fides, 3
Puerto Rico (U.S. Territory), 56
Purchaser,
    of estate or interest in
    land under Power of
    Attorney,
        entitlement to documents,
        30

Q

Qualifications,
    for office of Notary, 6-8
Qualified Certificate,
    definition under Electronic
    Commerce Act, 2000, 73
Qur'an (Koran),
    Muslim swearing on, 25

R

Raison d'être,
    of office of notary public, 9
Ratification,
    by Ireland of,
    Hague Convention of 5
        October 1961, 1, 44-47
    EC Convention of 25 May
        1987, 1, 48-49
Ready, Nigel, 3
Recognition of Electronic
    Contracts, 72
Recommendations of FATF *re*
    money-laundering, 69
Record of Notarial Act, 4, 34-36,
    65-69
    notary must keep, 4, 34,
    65-68
Refugee Act, 1996, 23
Registered Adoption Society,
    59-60
Register of Foreign Adoptions,
    58
Register or Protocol Book,
    for Ships Protests, 34
Registered Medical Practitioner,
    must execute Enduring

Power of Attorney
(EPA), 31
Registrar of Births etc., 18-19
Registrar of Supreme Court, 43,
   45, 48
Registrar of the Faculty of
   Notaries Public in Ireland, 8,
   87
Registrar of Wards of Court,
   Special Summons addressed
      to for registration of
      Enduring Power of
      Attorney, 32
Registration in Companies
   Registration Office (CRO) of
      Power of Attorney by
      company, 53
Registration of Enduring Power
   of Attorney in High Court,
   32
Registration Rights under
   Adoption Act, 58
Regulations,
   Enduring Powers of
      Attorney Regulations,
      1996, 31-32
   Enduring Powers of
      Attorney (Personal Care
      Decisions) Regulations,
      1996, 31
Regulations
   governing appointment of
      notaries public, 2, 6-7,
      9, 78-80, 88-89
Relevant Document,
   under Civil Law (Miscellane-
      ous Provisions) Bill, 2006,
      22-23

Remuneration of Attorney
   under Enduring Power of
   Attorney, 31
Reporting of Suspicious
   Transactions (Money-
   Laundering)
      to An Garda Síochána,
         65-66, 68-69
      to Revenue Commis-
         sioners, 65-66, 68-69
Representative, Diplomatic or
   Consular,
      in Legalisation
         procedure, 43-45
Requirement,
   to observe Code of Conduct,
      9
   to obtain a certificate of
      competency, 6-7
   to show need, dispensed
      with, 9
Requisites of a Ship Protest, 36
Residence,
   in Foreign Adoption, 58-59
Retention of Documents in
   Electronic Form, 74
Revocation of Power of
   Attorney, 27
   none (generally) of Enduring
      Power of Attorney, 32
Role of Notary Public in Foreign
   Adoption, 62-63
Romanian Adoptions, 57-58
Rubber Stamps (see under
   Notarial Accoutrements),
Rules of the Superior Courts
   (No. 2) of 1993, 2, 6-7, 9, 78

Direction of Chief Justice, under, 2, 6, 9, 79, 88, 89
Rules of the Superior Courts (No. 1), (Proof of Foreign Diplomatic, Consular and Public Documents), 1999, 49-51
Russian Adoptions, 63
Russian Federation, 56

S

Saint Helena, 56
Saint Kitts and Nevis, 56
Saint Lucia, 56
Saint Pierre and Miquelon, 56
Saint Vincent and The Grenadines, 56
Samoa, 56
San Marino, 56
Saturday,
   Bill payable on, 40-41
Scale of Fees,
   none for notaries, 16, 64
   Competition Act, 2002, 16
Seal of office of notary public, 4-5
Serbia and Montenegro, 56
Service provider,
   money-laundering obligations, 65-66, 68
   notary public as, 11-12, 65
   duty to establish identity of appearer, 10, 22-23, 65-67
Settled Land Act, 1882, 27
Seychelles, 56

Shatter, Alan, 58
Ship's Log,
   to be produced to notary, 36-37
Ship Protest,
   register to be kept, 34
   note of protest as interim measure, 35
Signature (and seal) of Notary Public,
   verification of by Apostille certificate, 44-45
   by Registrar, Supreme Court (Legalisation), 5, 20, 43, 44-47
Signature,
   electronic, 72-75
   verification data, 73
Signe Pardevant Moi, 19
Signing of Power of Attorney, 26-33
Signoque Meo Solito et Assueto Signavi, 20
Signs-manual, 20-21
Slovakia, 56
Slovenia, 56
Solicitors,
   Certificate supporting application for appointment as notary public, 9, 84
   Law Society Guidelines on Enduring Power of Attorney, 32
   Law Society Guidelines on money-laundering, 69
   may certify copy Power of Attorney, 30

Solomon Islands, 56
South Africa, 56
South Sandwich Islands, 56
Spain, 56
Special Summons,
   for registration of Enduring
      Power of Attorney, 32
   addressed to Registrar,
      Wards of Court, 32
Stamps (see Notarial
   Accoutrements),
Statement,
   of assets, in adoption, 60-61,
      102-103
   of reasons for declining
      certificate of competency,
      7, 79
Statute of Frauds (Ireland) 1695,
   74
Statutory Declarations Act, 1938,
   proposed amendment of,
      22-23
Statutory Declaration,
   of Translator, 13, 92-93
Stock Exchange Act, 1995,
   29-30
Stock Exchange Transaction,
   protection of transferee
      under Power of
      Attorney, 29
Suitability,
   of prospective adopters,
      59-60
Superior Court Rules, 2, 6-7, 78
Supreme Court Registrar,
   function in legalisation
      process, 43, 45, 48
Suriname, 56

Suspicious Transaction,
   money-laundering, 65, 68
   obligation to report, 65-69
Swaziland, 56
Sweden, 56
Swiss Confederation,
   identity card issued by, 23,
      100-101
Switzerland, 56

T

Taxation,
   implications for foreign
      property investor, 12-13,
      14, 94-95, 96-97
Telephone Call to Notary,
   seeking appointment, 62
   enquiry as to nature of
      business, documents,
      identification etc., 62, 67
Tenancy for Life,
   within Settled Land Acts,
      27
Terrorist Financing,
   monitored by FATF, 68-69
Testatum,
   of degree, diploma or
      certificate, 16
   verification of copy of, 16,
      98
Tests for Adoption,
   eligibility, 59-60
   suitability, 59-60
Text of Acknowledgement
   Letter, 14, 94-95
Tonga, 56
Transactions of Suspicious

Nature, 66
duty of service provider to
 report, 68
Translation of foreign
 language document, 13
Translator,
 services of, when required,
 13
 affidavit of, 13, 90-91
 declaration of, 13, 92-93
Travel Document,
 issued by Minister for Justice,
 Equality and Law
 Reform, 23
Travel Document
 (temporary) issued by the
 State in lieu of national
 passport, 23
Treatise on the Office of a
 Notary of England (Brooke),
 3
Trinidad and Tobago, 56
Trustee,
 non application of Power of
 Attorney to functions of,
 27
Turkey, 56
Turks and Caicos Islands, 56
Tuvalu, 56

U

Ukraine, 56, 63
Unbound pages,
 practice when notarising,
 15-16
 must be bound by notary, 15
Understanding,
 significance of document,
 notary's duty to be
 ensure, 10-11
Undertaking of Health Board
 Executive (HSE), in foreign
 adoption, intercountry
 adoption), 60-61
UNICTRAL, 72
United Kingdom, 40, 42
Virgin Islands (UK
 Territory), 56
United States of America,
 Nevada Forum on
 eLegalisation and
 eApostilles, 75
Virgin Islands (US
 Territory), 56
Uniqueness of Notary's
 Signature (see
 Signs-Manual), 20
Unter dach vor mir (Gm.), 19
Utility Bill,
 production of,
 to establish identity and
 place of residence, 10,
 67

V

Valid passport as evidence of
 identity, 10, 67
Vanuata, 56
Venezuela, 56
Verification,
 of Petition for Appointment
 as notary, 9
 Affidavit in, 9, 83
 of translation of foreign,

language document, 13
Affidavit, 13, 90
Statutory Declaration, 13, 92
of identity and legal capacity of appearer, 10-11
obligation of notary,11,14
Vessel,
Master of, to make Ship Protest, 34
Vietnam, 64
Virgin Islands (UK Territory), 56
Virgin Islands (US Territory), 56
Void,
agreement to fix notarial fees, 16
Competition Act, 2002, 16

W

Wallis and Futuna (Fr. Territory), 56
Walsh, Brendan (see Acknowledgements)
Walsh, David (see Acknowledgements)
Welfare System in Ireland,
affect on domestic adoption, 57
Wilful Blindness,
money-laundering transaction, 68
Wards of Court,
Enduring Power of Attorney,
Registrar of, a Notice Party, 32

Z

Zimbabwe, 56